Paradise Outlaws

> > > > > > > > **remembering the beats**

Also by John Tytell

The Living Theatre: Art, Exile and Outrage

Passionate Lives: D. H. Lawrence, F. Scott Fitzgerald, Henry Miller, Dylan Thomas, Sylvia Plath—in Love

Ezra Pound: The Solitary Volcano

Naked Angels: Lives and Literature of the Beat Generation

< < < < < O > > > > > > > >

Paradise Outlaws

> > > > > remembering the beats

John Tytell

photographs by Mellon

William Morrow and Company, Inc. ✳ New York

Library of Congress Cataloging-in-Publication Data
Tytell, John.
Paradise outlaws : remembering the beats
 John Tytell ; photographs by Mellon.—1st ed.
  p. cm.
Includes bibliographical references and index.
ISBN 0-688-16443-9
1. American literature—20th century—History and criticism.
2. Authors, American—20th century—Biography.
3. Beat generation.
I. Title
PS228.B6T93 1999
810.9'0054—dc21   99-18713
CIP

Printed in the United States of America

First Edition

1   2   3   4   5   6   7   8   9   10

BOOK DESIGN BY LOVEDOG STUDIO

www.williammorrow.com

This book is dedicated

to the memory of

Allen Ginsberg,

magnanimous mountain of

American poetry

Preface

The notion of paradise may be one of our ultimate fictions, but it still motivates action in the world. Writers such as Jack Kerouac, Allen Ginsberg, Lawrence Ferlinghetti, and Gary Snyder shared a unifying vision of a better future, of the possibilities for change in America. Kerouac's hero in *On the Road* is named Sal Paradise. In the beginning of his poem "Howl," Ginsberg refers to a place on Manhattan's Lower East Side he calls Para-dise Alley, though he qualifies "paradise" with the desperate connotations of drinking turpentine, making it seem more like a hopeful illusion, part of a romantic quest in a grimy neighborhood.

The Beats belong to a libertarian tradition that envisages an ideal—however romantic and unattainable—of the individual embracing personal freedom while resisting institutional values. The resulting conflict often made them outlaw artists, and the Beat story is one of risking sensibility for the sake of a new consciousness.

While the way the Beats saw the world made them outlaws, they also shared a populist perspective, a view of art that was unelitist, antihierarchical, egalitarian. They learned more on the street than in the academy. Most of them sought stylistic accessibility, and they all valued honesty as their first priority. Kerouac, William S. Burroughs, Gregory Corso, Jack Micheline, and Diane di Prima, among others, were more concerned with the raw guts of actual emotion and experience than veneration in the museum of literary culture.

Writers have rarely used the raw material of their lives as primally as the Beats. Burroughs made his addiction the subject of much of his fiction. Kerouac discovered the vulnerability that shaped his perceptions as a result of his experience of the road. The vagabond existence, living in destitution in Mexico, or on the boweries of New York City, Denver, and San Francisco, developed a sympathy that extended Kerouac's outlook. In a cynical age, such sympathy has a radically transformative potential, and Ginsberg shared in it, shaped as he was by the crucible of a childhood with his mad mother, Naomi.

The reader will quickly perceive that I choose a biographical perspective from which to view an especially exciting movement in our national literature, arguably the most significant since the much looser alliance of Ernest Hemingway, F. Scott Fitzgerald, and Gertrude Stein in Paris of the twenties.

Biography, however, is merely like the doorway through which one passes in order to reach a certain space, it is never an end of itself, and no one would bother discussing the Beats as literary figures unless some of them happened to create such signal expressions for our era as *On the Road, Howl,* and *Naked Lunch,* and a subsequent body of work that is still being read today.

To some extent I must confess that I am revisiting this material a quarter of a century after I wrote *Naked Angels,* one of the first histories of the Beats. At that time, most of the criticism the Beats had received was negative, much of it was quite condescending, and some of it was malicious and politically inspired.

Recently, I was asked to remember my experience teaching the Beats over a period of three decades. At the same time, I envisaged the series of essays reconsidering the Beat movement that forms the fabric of this book. While looking at my wife's photographs of the Beats, and at myself in some of them, I realized that the anecdotal reminders evoked by Mellon's photographs made them the emotional core of my project.

Indeed, the awareness of my own involvement with the Beats suggested a cohering thread with which to connect the pieces I wanted to write. Also, the recent deaths of Allen Ginsberg and Burroughs, of Herbert Huncke and Carl Solomon, provoked other more personal memories.

I regard this second chance at considering the Beats as remarkable, particularly since we are at the historical moment when some of them are becoming part of the canon and are viewed now more than ever as generational spokesmen of an era.

Acknowledgments

We are caught in an inescapable network of mutuality.

—Martin Luther King

By Way of Thanks

Many fine people have contributed to this book. Mellon and I are especially grateful to our editor, Ben Schafer, for his faith, enthusiasm, and discernment.

My first thanks go to Mellon for her photographs, support, and love. Ann Charters asked me to speak at the NYU Beat Conference in 1994, which was when I began work on "The Frozen Fifties." Both Joyce Johnson and Morris Dickstein were encouraging with the astute advice to include only recent writing in this book. Helen Kelly asked me to speak at the NYU Kerouac Conference in 1995, which was the seed for "Look for the Diamonds in the Sidewalk!" Nancy Comley, on her father's judicial stationery, counseled me to write the essay on Beat pedagogy, and Jennie Skerl helped shape it. Ann Douglas, viewing Mellon's photographs, told me I should organize a book about them. Bob Rosenthal allowed me to speak at the Ginsberg Memorial at St. Mark's Church, which was the beginning of the "Requiem for Ginsberg" included here. Barry Wallenstein and Susan Chang helped me question my assumptions. Franco Minganti persuaded me to speak about legacy at the Venice Film Festival in 1996. Ron Whitehead and Kees van Minnen invited me to Holland to speak about the Beats in 1997 and again in 1998.

Mellon would like to particularly thank all the people who allowed her to photograph them. Her gratitude goes to Klaus Moser for his beautiful prints and to Tom Ridinger for his intuitive eye. She is always grateful to Robert Frank, her osmotic mentor, for his encouragement and kindness along the road. Miles Barth gets a hearty thank you for exhibiting some of these photographs at the International Center of Photography in 1994. Richard O. Hire deserves special mention for his exquisite common sense and generosity. Thanks goes to Jack Barlev of Spectra Photo for doing a great job. Special thanks go to "Mommy-in," Lillian Roche Levenson, for her enduring love and faith in Mellon's ability, and to dear friends Richard Palmer, Marge Neikrug, Elly Davis, Shirley Cloyes, Joyce Johnson, Kazuko, Ken Stuart, and Bob Chard for their encouragement of and support for this project.

Finally, we both thank Fritz Metsch and Brian Mulligan for their sensitivity with the design of this book, Carin Goldberg for its cover, and Tom Nau for his concern with its production.

Contents

Returning to the Country for a Brief Visit

Reading Sung poems, I think of my poems to Neal
dead few years now, Jack underground
invisible -- their faces rise in my mind.
Did I write truthfully of them? In later times
I saw them little, not much difference they're dead.
They live in books and memory, strong as on earth

April 20, 1973   Allen Ginsberg

John Tytell with Shantih in the window,
Vermont, 1971.

In 1971, through a sparring partner of Norman Mailer's, Mellon found an abandoned, collapsing pre-Revolutionary farmhouse. The place was a giant cobweb crowded with broken furniture. It had one cold-water tap, a two-seater outhouse, forty-foot-long hand-hewn beams, and a feeling of ancient solidity and romance.

We planned to summer there quite simply, and would heat water to bathe in a big turkey pot. The house was situated on ten acres near the top of a hill with a spectacular fifty-mile view. During the rest of the year, we lived in the swarm of Manhattan, but on Colvin Hill there were no neighbors for a half mile in any direction. It was so silent that we could hear one of the four or five cars that would pass daily from several miles down the dirt road. Everyone in our family warned us that we were throwing our money down the hill. I thought this was a paradise of privacy, wildflowers, and drunken yellow finches, inebriates of the air that veered wildly in flight.

Surrounded by the bucolic beauty of this property, I began reading the Beats. My exploration of the literary gymnastics of a postmodernist pioneer like William Burroughs was balanced by a concern for the foundation of the farmhouse, huge boulders dragged into place by oxen two centuries earlier that had tumbled into my cellar.

I was an aspiring James scholar, trained in the New Criticism, which warned against the heresies of what was called the biographical fallacy and scrutinized text in a void exempt from the formative explanations of history. That ostrich approach seemed valid for undergraduates who needed to learn how to read carefully, but it was hardly useful for a historian. If they have something to say at all, writers tend to anticipate and reflect saliently defining aspects of their culture, and certainly their lives and how they lived them are part of the picture.

A key figure in this photograph is a king setter called Shantih, the Hindu term for peace. Anything but peaceful except when sleeping, Shantih was another balancing factor, a gorgeous redhead, a leaping, high-tempered animal who helped me roam the woods and fields. Peering through the old rough-framed window, next to the wide boards and lath of the uninsulated outside wall, Shantih poses in a rare moment of repose.

> > > > > > > > > >

A Biographical Journey

In fact, a biography cannot imitate life; it has to get rid of the chaos and the clutter; it rejects the habitual and the extraneous detail of our days; it rearranges its material; it tells a flowing story—something our lives never were.

—**Leon Edel,** *The Age of the Archive*

I   *The Renegade Path*

The history of any literary movement is at best a precarious adventure. Writers detest categories and groupings; like Faulkner claiming not to have read *Ulysses*, they ingeniously deny influences even as literary critics ascertain them. And since writers devote their waking moments to developing difference and dream about uniqueness, it is no wonder that they resist the linkings and contexts that can occasionally clarify their efforts.

The term "movement" applied to a chain of literary events, implies a tension between past tradition and a particular turn in the present. There was a time when events moved more slowly, when a single set of attitudes could dominate the literary community for long periods. So we can see the continuity of sensibility connecting Matthew Arnold to Wordsworth, for example, just as we can retrospectively recognize that when Arnold tells us in his preface to *Empedocles on Etna* that his own poetic voice has lost its authority, he is tacitly acknowledging the end of the romantic mood.

The twentieth century has been considerably less unified in literature as well as everything else, and literary movements, like celebratory fireworks in the night, are often transient spectacles. In our time, writers have paraded under the banners of Naturalism, Imagism, Vorticism, Modernism, and Surrealism, and they have affiliated themselves with groups like Bloomsbury or the Lost Generation.

Often an especially dynamic figure like Ezra Pound may be associated with several of these movements, and the interchangeability is an index of a tremendous diversity of artistic enterprise. In any literary movement, there exist the seminal forces, the genuine innovators, the impresarios, and the crowd of parrots. Imagism transformed modern poetry, but who, except for Pound or William Carlos Williams, was able to write a poem fulfilling Imagist principles that had any lasting value as a poem? The charisma of art is usually a seductive blandishment, as the followers of any literary style can attest, but imitation itself has its significance, and does exist as one sort of barometer of the informing power of any new view.

I offer these comments on the momentum of literary movement out of my interest in a recent American manifestation—the Beat Generation. This movement, controversially greeted, radical in its view of America and in its aesthetic, has had great cultural impact. Jack Kerouac, who named the movement and who has been called the spokesman of his generation, died in 1969 at the end of a turbulent decade that he, in part, helped to bring about even as he despised its excesses. While the movement involved a broad spectrum of writers in New York and San Francisco, in places like Kansas City, in small corners of the country like Reed College, and in centers of intellectual opinion like the University of Chicago, in this chapter I will focus exclusively on the lives and the aesthetic priorities of the three major figures: Burroughs, Kerouac, and Ginsberg.

They met in 1944 during a period of national crisis, and formed a sort of brotherhood animated by joie de vivre and grounded in despair: three young men living in New York City during the Second World War with intimacy, intensity, and an unusual reciprocity of interest. The oldest was William Seward Burroughs, a Harvard graduate who had come to New York out of a perverse inclination to consort with criminals. Jack Kerouac, from the provincial mill town of Lowell, Massachusetts, was attending Columbia University on a football scholarship. The youngest member of the group was Allen Ginsberg, an eagerly serious, aspiring poet studying with Mark Van Doren and Lionel Trilling at Columbia.

These three young men were almost as heterogeneous as the American nation: Burroughs, a crusty, genteel WASP with a cynical view of American possibilities; Kerouac, a shy observer, confused by the clash between his Catholic conditioning and the emerging hipster values he detected in New York City; and Ginsberg, a Jewish intellectual from New Jersey whose father wrote verse and whose mother had been confined in a madhouse.

Burroughs, who had read more, who had been psychoanalyzed, and who had traveled to Europe, became an informal mentor for Kerouac and Ginsberg, introducing them to books like Spengler's *The Decline of the West* and Wilhelm Reich's *The Cancer Biopathy*, and to writers like Céline, Cocteau, and Kafka. These men were surprisingly open with each other, and their discussions moved from books and ideas to more personal realities. Soon Burroughs was psychoanalyzing Ginsberg and initiating his younger friends with drugs like morphine and marijuana, which he had discovered through his underworld contacts. Before long, they were all sharing a large apartment near Columbia, communally experiencing the generational giddiness of Americans who first combined elements of surrealism and existentialism.

The rebellious camaraderie was partly a comfort in the presence of terrific pain. Burroughs was especially isolated and intent on repudiating his caste and its respectability. He was a marvelous raconteur, but a blocked writer who would not begin his first novel until his mid-thirties. All of them struggled with writing, and the problems they felt were connected to what they saw as a paralysis in the culture and the need to make new selves. Kerouac's French Canadian mother had a peasant's outlook and little sympathy for his ambitions. His father, dying of spleen cancer after the Second World War, saw his son as a failure while Kerouac spent years trying to justify himself with a sprawling apprenticeship in fiction, *The Town and the City*, a first novel influenced by Wolfe, Fitzgerald, and Hemingway. And Ginsberg, troubled by his mad mother, pressured by a cautiously conservative father, was anxious about his own homosexuality and dissatisfied with his ornate imitations of sixteenth-century verse, efforts that made him feel like a "ventriloquist of other voices."

Much of the pain and motive for rebellion was a mutual refusal to accept the shell-shocked values of postwar American culture. The war years had been a time of great national sacrifice; it seemed, afterward, that an enormous affluence was possible, but at certain costs. The gray-flannel-suit culture that William H. Whyte described in *The Organization Man* had little appeal for the Beats. Instead of repression, respectability, and careerism, their priorities were pleasure and freedom of expression. Kerouac spent his undergraduate nights at Minton's Playhouse, a jazz joint on 118th Street and St. Nicholas Avenue in Harlem, listening to Charlie Parker and Lester Young, trying to adapt the inspired spontaneous beat of black American music to his own prose rhythms. Ginsberg complained to his professor Mark Van Doren that Whitman and Henry Miller were ignored or disparaged by the Columbia academicians. Burroughs scorned American institutions and values, and in seeking out criminals and drugs was making of himself an untouchable. These men formed the vanguard of an underground generation in absolute revolt from unprecedented pressures for conformity, from the phlegmatically bovine dullness of the Eisenhower era. Instead of security, the Beats began a search for ecstasy, mystical experience, sexual release, and emotional honesty.

These were clearly unpopular ambitions during the Cold War years, a time of extraordinary insecurity and profound individual powerlessness, a perilous period in our history when old-fashioned notions of personal responsibility were being rationalized in the interests of corporate growth, when the catchwords were coordination and adjustment, and when the idea of individuality no longer seemed to matter.

The Beats responded to what they perceived as the stifling qualities of the fifties with a passionate roar. Each of their major works during this period, Ginsberg's *Howl*, Kerouac's *On the Road*, and Burroughs's *Naked Lunch*, caused publication difficulties or actual censorship proceedings: two thousand copies of *Howl* were seized by customs police in San Francisco in 1955 (the volume had been printed in England), and, like *Naked Lunch*, it could be released only after court tests. When *On the Road* appeared in 1957, it was vilified by many critics, who called it hedonistic, nihilistic, and onanistic. Critics especially deplored the delirious manners and reckless mores of headstrong characters who seemed able to sacrifice conventional bonds for the sake of change.

Apparently, some taboo had been threatened, some nerve in the cultural nexus had been exposed, some tacit agreement between artist and audience had been spurned, and the critics saw the young Beats as barbarians storming the literary citadel. Indeed, the Beats had returned to a romantic perspective (just about one hundred years after Arnold gave us his touchstone for the end of romanticism) in a time when expansive attitudes and lyrical expression were suspect, when literature was dominated by the narrow priorities of the "New Criticism": irony, strict formal adherence to literary convention, proper taste in subject matter. Postwar poetry was mandarin, decorative, diffident, difficult sometimes, it seemed, only for the sake of difficulty, ponderously burdened by the weight of T. S. Eliot's influence. A model is Robert Lowell's much-admired early volume *Lord Weary's Castle*—even its title connotes a fatigued elitism lost in a remote intellectual idyll that took shelter in abstraction.

The change in American poetry would begin with *Howl*. Instead of the mannered tradition of Henry James, the perspective that carefully applied fineness of sensibility and discrimination of feeling as a source of illumination about character and culture, the Beats followed the more rambunctiously renegade path of Whitman, Rimbaud, and Henry Miller. Regarding themselves as exiles within the culture, they rejected middle-class values for a bohemian libertarianism that romantically idealized freedom and spontaneity and saw, sometimes with paranoic terror, social controls at every corner.

The emancipation that so dissident a stance implies came as no sudden discovery, but as the result of a long history of travail and grief in the world. I want to chart some of the steps in this history—not for its sensational aspects, though Beat style was to use sensation, never to flee from it in shame, as a hieroglyph of life in a time of apathy—but to show how by transcending the values they opposed, they helped alter what they feared and so affected their age.

Of course, many modern artists find themselves in a situation antagonistic to culture. But the Beats were singular in their excess, given to more extreme gestures and actions than their contemporaries. The biographical focus with rebellious artists is always on the struggle with conditioning, the ways that the mores and thought patterns of a culture and one's parents subtly influence action or reaction and insinuate guilt with each departure from the circumscribed order. To put it simply, each of the Beats was willing to take enormous risks and to gamble with potentially dangerous experiences in order to transcend his conditioning. The routes, perhaps inevitably, were traditional and as venerable as the routes of some of the Old Testament prophets: travel, drugs, spiritual quest, and a profound argument with what it meant to be "sane" in a time when all definitions were shifting.

II   Brief Lives

No other contemporary writer endangered his mind and body as much as William Burroughs, who remained addicted to morphine, heroin, and other drugs from 1944 to 1958. Writers often choose their métier because of the power of personality and a desire to affect the world through the word; Burroughs, however, spent years in pursuit of obliteration. In one sense, he became a writer in spite of himself, and the drug experience that consumed him for so long, with its attendant deprivations and special transports, became his story.

Burroughs's childhood in St. Louis represented another extreme: the claustrophobic terrors of upper-class gentility. His grandfather had perfected the adding machine and founded the giant Burroughs Corporation, and that instilled a clear legacy for the entire family. Burroughs's father, as is often the case with children of fortune and power, was retiring and ineffectual; he spent his time collecting and finally selling antiques. Burroughs's mother smothered her son with an overdeveloped sense of Victorian propriety. Later on, Burroughs's fiction would emerge as a savagely inspired departure from his mother's mannered conventionality.

As an adolescent, Burroughs was fragile and sickly. Sent to a boarding school that stressed athletics, he instead read de Maupassant, Baudelaire, Wilde, and Gide, gradually developing an interest in crime. Remote, laconic, easily embarrassed by sentiment but attracted to other men, Burroughs attended Harvard during the Depression, studying literature, linguistics, and anthropology. After graduating from Harvard in 1936, Burroughs went to Europe, where he began medical studies in Vienna. He met a young Jewish woman who feared for her safety because of the Nazis; Burroughs married her so that he could bring her to the United States, where their arrangement of convenience was immediately dissolved.

War seemed imminent, and Burroughs tried to join the newly formed O.S.S. He had the right credentials and appropriate family connections—his uncle, Ivy Lee, was a good friend of William Donovan, who had organized the agency. While Burroughs passed all the intelligence tests, his application was denied when during his physical he admitted to having sliced off the tip of a finger with poultry shears to see what the sensation would be like. He later claimed that he had been jinxed by a former teacher at Harvard. The investigation of the limits of pain with the poultry shears and the conspiratorial intrigues of his subsequent fiction suggest that he would have become a master spy.

Burroughs was then drafted, but received a psychological discharge after six months and began psychoanalysis with a psychiatrist who had been analyzed by Freud. After his analysis, he drifted to Chicago to find the criminal elements that by then had begun to obsess him. He worked as a bartender, an exterminator, and a private detective, but encountered no gangsters in the city of Al Capone.

He did find some in New York City in 1944, just at the time when he met Kerouac and Ginsberg. His introduction to the world of petty criminality came through a Times Square hustler and hipster named Herbert Huncke. Burroughs rented a flat on the Lower East Side of Manhattan for Huncke, hoping to meet more underworld figures there. In the meantime, Huncke introduced him to morphine injections.

This was the time when Burroughs, Kerouac, and Ginsberg formed what I have already called their brotherhood, sharing a large apartment near Columbia with several women. One of them was Joan Vollmer Adams, a graduate student of journalism at Columbia who fell in love with Burroughs, left her husband, and lived with Burroughs for the next seven years.

After the war, Burroughs and Joan Vollmer—she dropped the Adams after her divorce—began to fear police apprehension because of their drug use, and they moved to a little farming community north of Houston, Texas. Burroughs's intentions were not particularly agricultural: he believed he could cultivate opium on his land so as to have the raw material for morphine and heroin.

At every step along the way, Burroughs was challenging authority and testing legal limits. While in Texas he became especially sensitive to the farm bureaucracy organized during the New Deal, and he chafed under its controls. He noticed the way in which such controls could be relaxed for the big farmers when they seasonally imported migrant laborers from Mexico, and he decided that since the law was so relative and so selectively applied, it had little inherent validity.

It is clear that Burroughs was following a path that would set him apart from the social compact binding men under government. In 1951, living in Mexico City and studying Mayan history and archaeology, he committed the act that effectively ruptured all remaining ties to family and state when he shot Joan Vollmer. Whether the act was or was not premeditated seems almost unimportant from a psychological perspective. The couple had a love/hate relationship, and Joan depended on Burroughs more than he needed her. They had a son, but Burroughs was homosexual; furthermore, in his fiction and later interviews, he expressed his misogyny.

The trial lasted almost a year. During this period, Burroughs finally broke through the barriers that had for so long blocked his dark vision, and he began writing *Junky*. The book had none of the experimental features of his subsequent work but naturalistically recorded the seedy world of addiction. Burroughs sent chapters to Allen Ginsberg in New York, who interested a friend named Carl Solomon whose uncle was a publisher. The book appeared under the pseudonym William Lee: Lee was his mother's maiden name. Kerouac had been encouraging Burroughs to write for years, but except for a sketch written at Harvard, he had done very little. Suddenly, as if the death of Joan Vollmer had somehow finally released him from the obligations of his conditioning, he was able to write.

Burroughs intensified his drug use after the trial. Leaving Mexico before the court's verdict, he voyaged into the backwaters of Columbia and Peru in search of *ayahuasca*, a South American psychedelic prepared and administered by tribal medicine men. He described some of his terrifying experiences in letters to Ginsberg, and his trip into the Conradian inferno seemed like some sort of purgation or expiation, as if the body itself was a treacherous vessel that had to succumb to natural law so that the vision could be released.

This is hardly offered as romantic rationalization. The fruit of Burroughs's perspective is evident in *Naked Lunch*, a major aesthetic advance in the form and content of the novel. Burroughs's addiction became even more serious after his South American travels. He moved to North Africa, where drugs and boys were available and cheap, and began taking notes on his own disintegration. These notes, some of them written during the delirium of drug addiction, became *Naked Lunch*, which itself is perhaps the most powerful artistic warning of the dangers of drugs in our time.

Naked Lunch, partly because of its censorship case, attracted great notice and affected the literary world. In a tremendous act of self-assertion, Burroughs broke his addiction to devote himself to writing. He had become the outsider incarnate, and his antagonism to the world would be expressed in a series of alarming apocalyptic auguries of Western breakdown. His telegraphic style and kaleidoscopic structure were clearly one early demonstration that fiction could move beyond Joyce, that a new postmodernist mode had begun.

One of the intriguing aspects of Burroughs's novels is the absence of any authorial presence, a character who might be seen as speaking his views. By inventing a panoply of changing characters and situating them in a mosaic architecture, by refusing to develop character in the ways a more traditional novelist might, Burroughs managed a harrowing invisibility. The act of writing, especially fiction, is so intimately a reflection of how a writer wants to see himself, a projection that may be idealized or exaggerated but is usually dependent on some significantly revealing distortion. In this respect, Burroughs follows the modernist line of T. S. Eliot, the position that requires effacement of personality. However, a literature of consistent invective and rage is itself a sufficient barometer of Burroughs's sensibility.

We all fashion personae for different occasions; some of us act to heighten our fantasies, even if only in some small token way. It is the business of fiction, however, to fabricate the fantasy, to weave an artifice, to embellish and empower what might otherwise seem quite ordinary. Part of the purpose of criticism is to clarify the distance between person and persona, a distance the artist often confuses or obscures. For any biographer, the mask, the projection, may reveal how an artist sees himself: is he rejected, self-loathing, aggressively proud, maniacally inspired? The possibilities are as vast as the range of personality, and they naturally determine the biographer's perspective.

In Kerouac's case, persona is more drastically present than in Burroughs's, more romantically pronounced and engaging, more enthusiastically the first-person "I" than the camera eye of the modernist aesthetic. His fiction suggests an almost insatiable quest for experience, at times beyond normal parameters, and always moving toward the release of feeling. The myth behind the books is that of the adventurer who knows no horizons, the American pioneer who heads for the territories, the man who when he reaches the top of the mountain tries to keep on climbing. Late in his life, when Kerouac was living in almost reclusive retirement in St. Petersburg, Florida, he was haunted by youths who would knock on his door expecting to be regaled by the characters he had once conceived. It is the kind of anomaly familiar to writers who have been too convincing with their fantasies.

That fantasy life began rather early for Kerouac. He started writing before his teenage years: family newsletters, journals, stories. His father was a small-time printer in Lowell, Massachusetts, who set type himself and taught his son to do it. Kerouac's parents were French Canadians, and they lived in the "Canuck" ghetto of Lowell until the Merrimack River flooded during the Depression and swamped Leo Kerouac's print shop.

As a young man in high school, Kerouac showed early signs of willfullness. He trained so hard for the track team that subsequently he developed thrombophlebitis, a clotting condition in the circulatory system. When he wanted to play football for Lowell High, the coach advised him he was not big enough for the team. Kerouac trained on his own and became a star running back, so good that he was offered an athletic scholarship by both Notre Dame and Columbia.

The Kerouacs were Catholic, and Gabrielle Ange, his mother, was cautious, conservative, and very religious. She wanted her son to attend Notre Dame. Leo, more impulsive and carefree, a man who had many friends in Lowell and loved the races and the barroom, wanted his son to be a football hero in New York. Kerouac realized that New York City offered opportunity for a writer; his mother saw writing only as a disreputable possibility.

Kerouac's life was as inconsistent and as contradictory as his literary career. After leaving Columbia University in the wake of a scandal—his friend Lucien Carr murdered a man who had attempted to assault him sexually—and joining the merchant marine during the war, Kerouac spent five years toiling on his first novel, *The Town and the City*, which appeared in 1950 to favorable reviews but limited sales. The book was written in a conventional style. Kerouac was still learning how to write fiction, but he knew how important it was to discover a new form and a new way of storytelling.

His catalyst was another young friend named Neal Cassady, a reform school delinquent who read Proust and also wanted to become a writer. Cassady, who became a model of living to the fullest for the Beats, sent Kerouac a forty-page, single-spaced, unpunctuated letter describing his sexual exploits. Kerouac saw in its colloquial naturalness of expression an energy that could transform his own prose.

Cassady was an indefatigable conversationalist, a talker of inexhaustible velocity who encouraged Kerouac to discover the virtues of the open road. Actually, Kerouac came to hate the vulnerability of the hitchhiking that he later popularized and much preferred the security of the Greyhound bus, but he allowed himself to be lured from his worktable on many occasions because he realized that Cassady had become his subject. However, the writer who made a myth out of the adventures of his gregarious friends spent most of his time living with his mother in a lower-middle-class section of Queens. And after each trip to Cassady's hometown of Denver, to Mexico to visit Burroughs, to California when Cassady moved there, Kerouac would return to the sanctuary of his mother's kitchen to assimilate his experiences and record them.

He had vowed as a Catholic to his dying father that he would always protect his mother, and he remained faithful to that vow, abruptly ending his first two marriages because of it, and marrying again near the end of his short life the sister of a childhood friend who had died in the war, a nurse whom he knew would continue to care for his mother if he died before her. Since Kerouac was largely responsible for creating an interest in Buddhism during the sixties (because of his novel *The Dharma Bums*), a view that accepts the inevitability of suffering and the importance of detachment, the tie to his mother represents yet another aspect of contradiction.

Kerouac's life presents problems for any biographer because he claimed to write directly from experience, without revision (which he saw as a subtle form of censorship) or other altering of the actual. To an amazing extent he succeeded, but the game of fiction with the distorting roles of memory and ego projection inevitably affects any historical record. As a man, Kerouac was afflicted with deep feelings of loss and estrangement; as a writer, he created a spectacle of manic union, merging, identification in love. So the fiction was the exact reverse of the man. The power of the book for which he became famous, *On the Road*, depends much more on Kerouac's mythmaking ability than on any confessional imperative. What his audience really cared about was a version of Huck Finn who actually did light out for the territories to find a dream of lost freedom and innocence. What made that audience feel his story was the manner in which Kerouac set it down, with a rhythmic, rhapsodically lyrical sweep and an excited American vernacular.

On the Road was written in a three-week burst of inspiration in 1951, but published only in 1957 after the Lost Generation writer Malcolm Cowley succeeded in convincing the editors at Viking Press that Kerouac had written an important book. During the six years that Kerouac had to wait for the acceptance and publication of *On the Road*, he wrote another dozen books. While he was convinced of his own genius, he felt it would not be recognized in his time.

One act that seems suggestive of Kerouac's distress at this time was his decision to work as a lookout for the Forest Service, spending two months on the top of a desolate mountain peak in Washington, writing, meditating, generally living like a monk in communion with the starry universe. Kerouac had accepted his anonymity and weathered it with a kind of homespun Buddhist nature worship.

When *On the Road* appeared, it aroused a storm of controversy and publicity for which Kerouac was entirely unprepared. Some self-destructive inclination, which perhaps is the edge to living for the sake of intense experience anyway, caused him to drink more and more heavily, and the alcoholism warped him, soured his writing, closed him to the very friends who had once so filled him with a sense of possibility. Like Melville, Kerouac retreated from the world. In 1969, at the age of forty-seven, consumed by his drinking, bitter, angry, and still confused, his body collapsed and he died of abdominal hemorrhaging.

Allen Ginsberg led a life as full of vicissitude as Kerouac's. When he met Kerouac and Burroughs, he was full of nervous intensity and an eagerness to be accepted. His own childhood, as his poem "Kaddish" attests, had been scarred by a mother whose paranoia was so developed she believed that Roosevelt was eavesdropping on her secret thoughts. Naomi Ginsberg became an inmate of mental institutions and eventually received a frontal lobotomy. She represented, Kerouac noted in a letter, the psychic wound that made Ginsberg a poet. Ginsberg's father, Louis, a high school English teacher and poet, encouraged his son to follow convention in his life as well as in his poetry. Ginsberg devoted his life to a refutation of that paternal advice.

At Columbia University, Ginsberg won literary prizes but was dissatisfied by what he considered to be the imitative, manneristic inferiority of his poetry. He was also anxious and unsure about his homosexuality. He felt that his poetic ambitions would never be realized unless he received psychiatric assistance. After graduating from Columbia in 1948, he was galvanized by an auditory hallucination of William Blake's voice, an experience that terrified him as much as it excited him to the possibility of participating in the prophetic tradition of poetry.

Through a Chaplinesque involvement with Herbert Huncke and a band of petty thieves, Ginsberg spent almost a year at Columbia Psychiatric Institute, sent there instead of to prison when his former teacher, the critic Lionel Trilling, interceded on his behalf. Later he would receive more treatment at the Langley-Porter Clinic in San Francisco.

The lesson that he took from all his analysis was what Burroughs had told him when he performed an amateur analysis during the first year of their friendship: to accept himself as he was, without shame. This realization led, in San Francisco in 1955, to the spontaneous transcription in the style Kerouac had taught him which we know as *Howl*—a brilliant and overwhelming release of sheer feeling and rhythm that changed the direction of American poetry. At that time, Ginsberg met Peter Orlovsky, a younger man, with whom he lived for over three decades.

During the sixties, Ginsberg continued to write poems, appearing frequently before large gatherings and soon gaining the reputation of being the most powerful reader of poetry since Dylan Thomas. Much more overt politically than either Burroughs or Kerouac, he devoted himself to the effort against the war in Vietnam, and in *The Fall of America* (1974) he documented the internal consequences of that era. He traveled to India, mixing morphine with guru searches and learning to chant mantras. He visited Czechoslovakia and Cuba, and was expelled from both; the libertarian consciousness that he advocated is anathema for any totalitarian regime. Returning to the United States, he participated in the psychedelic movement.

Ginsberg seemed to be simultaneously reaching in a number of directions, all of which affected what he was writing: living on a farm in upstate New York, learning to make music with Bob Dylan, intensifying his Buddhist study and meditation. He consistently expanded the frontiers for poetry by experimenting with blues improvisations and Blakean songs capable of both tender harmony and unprecedented raw revelation.

Ginsberg's imperative was always to transform normative consciousness so as to shock free a visionary possibility, and the kind of confrontational, personal politics he pursued was a crucial factor in discovering such a vision. Indeed, what some might call Ginsberg's outrageousness can be seen as the paradigm of Beat consciousness, devoted to the expression of direct feeling of love or fear, no matter what the cost to public image or convention.

III   My Beat Beginnings

I offer these portraits as an instance of passionate literary moment in our time. Part of the difficulty in presenting them is that excess is often mistrusted and usually feared more than admired. During the fifties, a time of many silent omissions, the Beat polemic was release. The Beats' politics were not leftist as much as libertarian, and their purpose was to rouse, to challenge, to question the changes caused by the new technologies, to help Americans remember that this too was a place where people could dream of a better future.

Their visions of that future occurred as the consequence of a struggle with their own conditioning at great psychic cost. In Kerouac's case, the struggle depleted his creative energies before he was forty, although he continued to live in considerable torment for another seven years. The value of such suffering for the community, however, is whatever spiritual insight may ensue as art, particularly if the sufferer seeks to record the changes along the way. In this sense, Kerouac shares a communion of perception with Burroughs and Ginsberg.

When I began my work on the writers of the Beat Generation, as a young scholar who had written about Henry James and Ford Madox Ford, about Baron Corvo and Richard Crashaw, there was virtually nothing useful on the subject. Although it does seem difficult to believe, as late as the end of the 1960s the Beats were regarded more as rabble-rousers than writers of merit. While there had been enormous coverage in the media, in magazines like *Time* and *Life*, it was more like bearbaiting than criticism, a taunting ridicule of a lifestyle that seemed incomprehensible or incorrigible to many whose values had been formed during the yawning complacency of what I call "the frozen fifties."

While completing a doctoral thesis on Henry James's enormous changes in narrative strategy during the 1890s, I edited a book for Harper &

Row called *The American Experience: A Radical Reader*, perhaps the first collection of countercultural writing. The book represented an opposite extreme from the mannered gentility of Henry James; it was controversial because it included essays and manifestoes by such figures as Norman Mailer, Timothy Leary, Malcolm X, and Lenny Bruce as well as Ginsberg.

Emerging from the graduate program at New York University in 1968, I reviewed Kerouac's last novel, *Vanity of Dulouz*, for *The Catholic World*, and Bruce Cook's *The Beat Generation*, a thin, insubstantial overview of the Beats, for *Commonweal*. While I deplored the journalistic superficiality and sensationalism of Cook's book, I was intrigued by some of the interview material he presented.

In 1970, I was an untenured assistant professor in an English department with lots of star players at Queens College, considered the jewel of the City University of New York. Many of the young people of Queens were finally outraged by the endless war in Southeast Asia, and they were demanding changes, holding sit-ins in corridors and occupying buildings, refusing to take spring-semester final exams. I saw over a hundred of them, singing "We Shall Overcome" with an inebriated revolutionary passion, impeding rush-hour traffic on the boiling pavement of the Long Island Expressway until the police arrived.

To placate the students, to "civilize" them into listening again in terms of the only discourse universities can accept, the college instituted what it called "The Last Lecture Series" and invited its most prominent faculty to address students as if this were a final opportunity to say something meaningful in a university setting.

I was flattered to be one of the dozen faculty asked to speak—I'm sure it was because of the notoriety associated with my *Radical Reader*. I knew I could not interest agitated students in the highly mannered leisure-class morality of Henry James. So I decided to talk about the Beats, sensing that they represented the first spokesmen of a generational divide that was what had caused all the student turbulence in the first place.

As a career move, my choice of subject may have been a bit perverse. In the academy, as everywhere else, one is supposed to placate the ruling powers with lullabies of reassurance. Talking about Ginsberg's and Burroughs's predictions of the fall of America could hardly promise that.

Spoken words are transient—as Bob Dylan sings, they are "blowin' in the wind." I knew I had to write an essay, to articulate my observations with the stability of the written word. I called what I wrote "The Beat Generation and the Continuing American Revolution."

What the Beats needed most in 1970 was intellectual credibility in the world of letters. The essay could have gone to *Harper's* or to *Esquire*, but I chose *The American Scholar*, a far more venerable magazine published by Phi Beta Kappa, the most prestigious honor society in America. The magazine kept the piece for a very long time, almost eight months, and I later learned there had been a ferocious in-house squabble about whether it should be printed.

When it appeared, in the spring of 1973, I sent it to Allen Ginsberg. He responded enthusiastically, declaring that my essay would change the reputation of the Beats, and he sent copies to William Burroughs, John Clellon Holmes, Carl Solomon, and Herbert Huncke. They were all willing to be interviewed, and Holmes offered to assist me with letters and journals.

I also met Joyce Johnson, who had been Kerouac's lover in 1957, the year *On the Road* appeared. She was a senior editor at McGraw-Hill, which then still had an active trade division, and was editing Jack Kerouac's *Visions of Cody*. Graciously receptive but a demanding editor, she offered me a contract for *Naked Angels*.

I was fortunate to be living in New York City, since Allen Ginsberg had deposited his letters and papers as well as whatever he had saved of Kerouac's and Burroughs's at Columbia University. The collection, however, seemed a reflection of how Columbia (and, in fact, America) regarded the Beats—it was a chaotic quagmire without collation or chronology, a disorder of undated notes and fading, unprotected letters stuffed in shoe boxes.

After reading this material, and the university collections like the one at the Humanities Research Center in Austin, and using private collections like the one owned by Kerouac's friend John Clellon Holmes, I knew enough to begin interviewing various Beat writers. What I had to learn was how to ask a question (often despite the feeling that I was just blundering into the trivial) that could serve to break through the surface of events as they inevitably become fogged in time and memory, and how to overcome mistrust of the man asking the questions.

I suppose my greatest luck was in locating the lesser figures in the Beat group. I reached Huncke only through a fluke of friendship and after enough negotiation to end a small war. Although he wanted to talk, he had been in prison and was suspicious. No one had interviewed him previously, and although he had appeared as a fictional character in Burroughs's work and in Kerouac's, he was still then a historical cipher.

Lucien Carr was even more problematic. He tried to get me drunk to avoid any questions when I met him in a bar near the *Daily News* building, where he worked as an editor at United Press International. He began to confide in me only after a former student, a New York City fireman in uniform, approached me dangling at the bar on my fourth martini with a question about Franz Kafka. At that point, of course, I was three sheets to the wind and barely able to answer, much less pursue the evasive Mr. Carr, though I did try through several more martinis.

I had a warmer reception from John Clellon Holmes, who opened his home to me and my wife, offering grace and hospitality as well as his own journals and correspondence. There was even more warmth and a continuing friendship with Carl Solomon, whom Ginsberg had met at Columbia Psychiatric Institute, and who then spent eight years in other institutions. I saw him regularly, and he was forever afflicted and dependent on tranquilizers, always asking the same unanswerable questions one would expect to read only in a novel by Dostoevsky.

There was a surfeit of material, but my real lesson was the understanding that not all of it could be used without losing my readers in an avalanche of detail. It was only after completing a first draft of *Naked Angels* that I was able to eliminate entire chapters on poets like Gary Snyder, Lawrence Ferlinghetti, and Gregory Corso, which blurred my perspective. What Burroughs, Kerouac, and Ginsberg had begun in New York City near the end of the Second World War eventually would affect writers all over America. The decision to focus on them was not reached without circumspection—for one thing, the Puritan in me shuddered at rejecting months of my own work—but it did respond to a clear chronological and geographical validity.

What was much more difficult was the fact of my own conditioning, the years of reading more classical forms of expression, which had helped to form my taste as well as that of the Western world, and an academic process that reveres the past while almost always condescending to the present. It is easier to idealize the dead; the living can be querulous.

As a graduate student, I had been warned by Oscar Cargill, a well-known Americanist, that positions teaching modern or especially contemporary literature were practically unobtainable, and that it would be wiser for me to devote my studious ambitions to the nineteenth century. Professor Cargill was right, since contemporary literature, like creative writing, as a subject for university study was another postwar phenomenon that was only beginning to catch on. Later, when I went to Columbia University to ask Lionel Trilling about his former students Ginsberg and Kerouac, he informed me that in their time no one got past the Victorians in literature classes, and Matthew Arnold was considered modern.

Another barrier was a general disdain among the academic critics for the Beats. Merely by their personal appearances, the Beats violated the idea of literary decorum that seemed so important in the fifties. Ginsberg, for example, shaggy and bearded, once undressed after reading *Howl* in answer to an irate questioning professor who wanted to know what he meant by "nakedness." Kerouac would wear open-necked, red-checkered lumberjack shirts instead of a coat and tie when he read from his work, and presented himself more as woodsman than wordsman. As a result, few critics (even the more rebellious ones like Leslie Fiedler) had the courage to take seriously what the Beats set down in print. There was little sympathy, for example, for the sheer absurdity causing the improvised playfulness evident in Robert Frank's film *Pull My Daisy*, which encouraged the goofy antics of Ginsberg and Corso to the music of Kerouac's narration.

In fifties America, there was no precedent for writers who psychoanalyzed each other, or who so openly used their experiences with drugs or homosexuality as subject matter. Such scandals as Verlaine's shooting and seriously wounding Rimbaud in Belgium seemed unmentionable in American art, as if the critics believed that the actual passions of life were somehow separate from what writers described. The late fifties, when *Howl*, *On the Road*, and *Naked Lunch* appeared, have been characterized by Ginsberg as a time vexed by the "syndrome of shutdown," but it was apparent that the genteel strictures that had for so long governed public taste and publishing were ready to be challenged. In 1960, when I was still an eager undergraduate, two events signaled that change: the ransacking of the papers and persons of the House Un-American Activities Committee in San Francisco by an unruly mob, and the attempted publication of *Tropic of Cancer* (to the accompaniment of a court case in each state).

Considering the public reception of the Beats in the fifties, what was interesting to me was that the established critics seemed threatened by the quality and character of their writing. Some were appalled, as poet and New Critic Allen Tate was, by Burroughs's scatological sexuality, his scenes of sadistic terror presented in a scary moral vacuum with what must have seemed gratuitous shocks. Others impugned Kerouac's ebullience, his romantic declaration that the writer should accept his original notation, that revision was a subtle form of self-censorship, an accommodation to satisfy public taste. Retrospectively, we can understand why Kerouac caused such an uproar, why he was so suspected and outcast, why Diana Trilling condescendingly dismissed her husband's former student for what she termed the "infantile camaraderie" of *On the Road*, why Herbert Gold jealously called Kerouac a "Pseudo-Hipster" in *The Nation*, or why Truman Capote quipped that Kerouac's writing was only typewriting. Fundamentally, the problem was one of decorum, so when Randall Jarrell (who would later commit suicide by stepping in front of a car) accepted his National Book Award in 1960, he went out of his way to castigate Kerouac, arguing that the quality of personal revelation in *On the Road* was more suitable for a successful psychoanalysis than for fiction.

As a graduate student, reading Northrop Frye or R. P. Blackmur on James, schooled in the fastidious euphonics of the New Criticism, I was taught to believe that literary credibility was in large part a function of critical authority. But the Beat writers were almost universally deplored and, by some, clearly despised. The critics saw them as philistines without a viable literary past, as a species of distasteful and aberrant contemporary anomaly. The early reviews of *Howl*, the first major book published by a Beat author, document this. John Hollander, writing about his own Columbia classmate in a spirit of evident distrust for what he saw as modish avant-garde posturing, complained in *Partisan Review* of "the utter lack of decorum of any kind in this dreadful little volume." James Dickey, in *Sewanee Review*, established Ginsberg as the tower of contemporary Babel, finding the poem full of meaningless utterance. Ginsberg's own self-assumed role of media clown in the sixties did little to redeem or improve this reputation. For some time, the critics could not fathom the poetic precedents for his long lines, just as they were put off by his blatant message of apocalypse, and the hysterically strident condemnation of the very institutions that fostered their efforts.

Over time, as the Beats became established as the heroes of an alternative culture, this reputation began to change. Recently, portions of Kerouac's unpublished notebooks have appeared in magazines like *The New Yorker* and *The Atlantic Monthly*, signs of unabated interest in his writing. His books have been brought back into print (with *On the Road* selling more than sixty thousand copies annually) while the works of some of those who formerly disparaged him are forgotten. The Beat phenomenon has now persisted for over half a century. By resisting narrow Puritan rigidities and by articulating the dangers of the national security state, the Beats have had a considerable impact on American mores and manners. These are matters whose consequences I hope to assess in the following chapters of this book.

I sent Allen Ginsberg my *American Scholar* piece "The Beat Generation and the American Revolution," which he immediately praised, recognizing that it was the most affirmative essay that had been written about the Beats, and that it could represent a turning point in their reputation. Perhaps because his father had been a minor poet without a real audience, and his mentor William Carlos Williams's place in American letters had been established posthumously, Ginsberg was very aware of literary reputation and did what he could to rectify the popular impression that the Beats were reckless wordslingers.

Ginsberg invited me to his farm in Cherry Valley, just south of Cooperstown, for a week around Labor Day in 1973. Mellon and I drove there from Vermont in an Austin Mini, a tiny, square breadbox of a car, which we had reupholstered in a yellow fabric with purple polka dots. The car featured thirteen upside-down American flag decals decorating a dent in the rear. The cockeyed flags were a statement of sorts, and they got us stopped occasionally by police.

The first thing Allen asked me as I emerged from my car was whether we had met previously. If there was a touch of suspicion in his query, I understood that it came from an ancient antipathy between the artist and the biographer, who so often represents a betrayal by oversimplifying the poet's pure vision.

I see a familial resemblance in the photograph, and the beards, as in an old Smith Brothers advertisement for Jewish cough syrup, do look similar, untrimmed and earthy in the untrammeled spirit still evident in the early 1970s. If I seem placid and self-contained, that was merely an exhausted pose for the click of the shutter.

Full of excitement and curiosity, I released a lot of energy bending and stooping in the vegetable patch that week, picking beans and tomatoes with Allen. I had a little notebook in my back pocket in which I would scribble with dirt-soaked fingers while Allen answered some of my questions about Beat history or Burroughs's and Kerouac's fiction.

There was something unpretentious and natural about the process. My purpose was intellectual, the discovery of a literary dynamic that had occurred decades earlier, which was already filtered and perhaps fogged by memory and time. History could nourish the imagination, and aesthetics seemed more exotic than the squash and cucumbers at my feet. Harvesting the vegetables, however, grounded me, a reminder of the real work ahead.

Peter Orlovsky in Basil, Cherry Valley, 1973.

"Be crazy dumbsaint of the mind" Jack Kerouac declared as one of his principles in "Essentials of Spontaneous Prose." Allen Ginsberg kept this list posted on his bedstead in San Francisco in 1955, the time of the composition of *Howl*. Peter Orlovsky, with his outrageously eccentric personal lyrics, was surely one of those "dumbsaints," and Kerouac named him Simon Darlovsky in *Desolation Angels*.

Peter was good with his hands. When I met him in Cherry Valley, he was hammering together a bedframe for Mellon and me to sleep in during our visit. Vigorous, handsome, Peter was a shy, moody man. I felt an immediate connection when he told me that as a young man he had worked as a field laborer on some of the last farmland in Queens, now adjacent to the campus at Queens College in New York where I have taught for over three decades.

Peter roared around the Cherry Valley farm in a tractor as he worked the land, mended fences, cut and stacked cords of wood, canned tomatoes, and pickled beets.

One of the reasons Allen had purchased the ninety-acre farm was Peter's reliance on methedrine, which he would score in the East Village. During the 1960s, Allen constantly traveled throughout the United States and Europe, and when he was away, Peter could be tempted. The farm represented health and recovery and Allen's rule was no drugs or alcohol.

Peter's radiant masculine sexuality and his intense silence reminded Mellon of Mellors in *Lady Chatterley's Lover.* Her photograph of Peter in a basil patch suggests some of the frank Dionysian beauty that attracted Allen to his lifetime companion when he saw Robert LaVigne's full-sized nude study of Peter in San Francisco in 1954. When they met a few moments later and gazed into each other's eyes, Ginsberg felt a "celestial cold fire" that illuminated everything.

Revealing a tender side underneath a patina of macho gruffness, Peter began writing poems in 1957 because of Allen's influence, although he never regarded himself primarily as a poet. Their union, and Richard Avedon's nude photograph of the two of them with their arms around each other, did much to popularize a gay lifestyle when it was widely circulated as a poster in the 1960s, even though Peter was essentially heterosexual. His sexual connection to Allen had faded by the time the poster appeared.

Julius and Peter Orlovsky, Cherry Valley, 1973.

Oleg Orlovsky, a cadet in the czar's army and later a guard at the Winter Palace during the Russian Revolution, emigrated to America in 1921. He married Katherine Schwarten, an aspiring writer encouraged by Dorothy Parker, who abandoned her literary ambitions when her face was partially paralyzed and she lost her hearing after a botched ear operation.

Oleg painted designs on ties, and earned a precarious living. With their five children, the Orlovskys lived in a converted chicken coop in Northport, Long Island (where Jack Kerouac later lived for a time), in conditions of considerable poverty. During the war, his parents separated and the children moved with their mother to Queens. When he was seventeen, a high school senior, Peter's mother told him he was good-looking enough to support himself.

Peter worked as an attendant at Creedmore State Mental Hospital in Jamaica, caring for senile and demented patients. A few years later, he was discharged from the army after telling a government psychiatrist, in an epiphany that could have been conceived by Gertrude Stein, that "an army is an army against love." He had been asked to clean his barracks, and instead threw out weapons, helmets, and whatever he found ugly, and painted flowers on the lockers.

Julius, Peter's older brother, shown in the photograph with a machete in his right hand, had been institutionalized as a child and experienced the ravages of mental illness during his entire life. He did not speak for fourteen years, convinced that all the evil in the universe emanated from his body and mouth. In 1965, diagnosed as a catatonic schizophrenic, he was released into Peter's care. Robert Frank made a sympathetic film called *Me and My Brother* about their relationship.

A poignantly mute figure, passive, beat, simultaneously ominous and innocent, Julius spent lots of time with Peter and another brother named Lafcadio in Cherry Valley during the 1970s in an attempt to restore health.

(continued)

Carl Solomon, Ginsberg, Orlovsky, John Tytell, and tomatoes, 1973.

(continued)

Many years later, a strange coincidence occurred that deepened my connection with Peter. In 1982, when my mother was succumbing to an eight-year battle with leukemia, she was in Mount Sinai Hospital in Manhattan. Oleg was recovering from an operation in a room down the hall. I visited him, and Peter and Allen visited my mother. I felt so grateful because the visits seemed to fortify my mom with the courage to face an uncertain future.

The visits had an extra significance. I chose writing as a young man because my mother, a student of Pearl Buck, struggled to write fiction and plays. But her native language was French and she was insecure about English. When I returned from school, she would ask me to read what she wrote to determine whether the diction sounded sufficiently American. Seeing my mother poised against her typewriter in a small room off the kitchen, trying to transform ideas and feelings into words, fascinated and formed me.

Allen Ginsberg in his Cherry Valley kitchen, 1973.

Conceived of as a refuge from a culture of overconsumption, Allen's farm had no electricity, and everything on it was grown organically. The kitchen was the communal center of the farm, and Allen accommodated various indigent poets and their families there over the years.

I remember Mellon's apprehension about our visit. She feared that it might be an uncomfortable experience with a group of gay, misogynist men. She had just photographed Ralph Lauren's men's and women's collections. Mellon was very young, and just entering a world that was very different from the Beats'.

In Cherry Valley, she had to transform her vision entirely. Allen observed her nervous excitement, and he suggested that she meditate. "Just do it!" he said. "Sit down with your legs crossed, pick a spot twenty inches away from your nose, and follow your breath."

Allen's kindly manner and the warmth of the kitchen reassured her. It was redolent with herbs and spices, and smells of the tomatoes and vegetables Peter was canning. Allen baked an apple pie with apples gathered on the farm, and the delicious winy odor permeated everything.

There were huge piles of vegetables everywhere. I asked Peter what happened to any surplus, and he explained it was donated to a Zen monastery in nearby Sharon Springs.

William Burroughs in front
of the West End bar, 1974.

The West End was a dark, cavernous place with a horseshoe bar, where Columbia University students would drink or eat a quick cafeteria meal from the steam table. Near the end of the Second World War, Ginsberg, Kerouac, and Burroughs would meet Lucien Carr and other friends there.

Except for a few brief periods, Burroughs had been out of New York for twenty-five years, living as an expatriate in Mexico, Colombia, Tangier, Paris, and London. He returned to read at the West End, where in some sense the Beat story began.

Burroughs looked like a British banker and read with a formal reserve that contradicted the hilarious excesses of his characters. His precise, deadpan dry delivery seemed like a sober cover for the extremities he described. This was one of the first in a series of over 150 readings, some to very large audiences over the next ten years.

In another photograph that Mellon took that afternoon just before the reading began, Burroughs is leaning on the front of an upright piano, staring into the flame of an old kerosene lantern. Her eye caught a noose in the way the cords of a venetian blind drape behind Burroughs's shoulder. It is a subtle evocation of the hanging figures in the notorious orgasmic death scenes repeated throughout *Naked Lunch*.

Burroughs with noose, 1974.

Carl Solomon epitomizes the Beat notion of the writer as *outcast*. Commemorated in "Howl" as a victim of mental suffering—he received more than seventy insulin and electric shock treatments in eight years of hospitalization—he was called a "lunatic saint" by his friends.

Feeling entirely obligated to fulfill their expectations, Solomon became the world's intellectual antagonist. His first book, *Mishaps, Perhaps*, is polemical, impish and impious, outrageously funny, and a reminder of the sort of suffering society sometimes offers to unconventional minds who would refute its dogmas and taboos.

"Howl" is dedicated to Carl Solomon, and partly inspired by some of his more volatile actions. His presence combined a naive idealism, an utter sincerity, an ardor for argument that was redeemed by an instinct for the absurd, and some rare flashes of the kind of quick rage one finds in Blake's portraits of children.

The anger was greater when Allen Ginsberg first met Carl, who was being wheeled into a ward at Columbia Psychiatric Institute after an insulin shock treatment—but Carl still had the wit to emerge from his coma with a Dostoevskian repartee. Much of Carl's fury was dissipated during his years of residence at Pilgrim State Hospital on Long Island. The opening line of "Howl," "I saw the best minds of my generation destroyed by madness," evokes Carl's attempts to reach far beyond the incipient apathy of the postwar years for some otherworld of inspiration and excitement.

Mellon's photograph suggests a stiff awkwardness—Carl seems uneasy, squeezed, cornered. He told me that he had twice pretty much talked his way into the madhouse. Carl made me into a maternal figure in our ensuing friendship, and he would confide his troubles. Sometimes I would be frightened by his vehement rages, often inspired by what I considered an innocuous remark.

Dependent on a life diet of tranquilizers, Solomon worked as a messenger. I encouraged him to write for *American Book Review*, and gradually persuaded him to work on another book and gave him its title, *Emergency Messages*—reflecting both his occupation and the urgent tone of some of his communications. It seemed so sad that the man who had accepted, edited, and prefaced Burroughs's first book, *Junky,* would be relegated to walking sidewalks. But Carl, the son of a house painter, had no pretentions and saw himself as an intellectual of the sidewalks, independent of pedigree and free of affectation.

Nash

Holmes shared a special relationship with Jack Kerouac, and he was the first person to read the manuscript of *On the Road*. Their friendship began in the years immediately following the Second World War, with Kerouac showing Holmes the journal and notebook drafts of a novel that he was arduously composing into his first published book, *The Town and the City*.

Holmes was eager to learn about the new hip world that Kerouac inhabited, and its strangely illuminated figures—Allen Ginsberg, William Burroughs, and Herbert Huncke. Holmes yearned to capture some of the freedom from more traditional allegiances that these men represented. For Kerouac, Holmes was a bedrock of value, a man whose judgment was dependable because he retained a sure sense of what was right in an exceptionally volatile environment.

Kerouac confided in him because Holmes, too, was ready to abandon the old answers that would no longer work, but even more because Holmes was a serious spirit, a man genuinely struggling in his art and in his life to discover valid responses in an anxious time without simply escaping into a flagellant nihilism. To Kerouac, Holmes was a marker, a buoy, a man on the border between straight and hip, past and present, a man with the sensitivity to make discriminations and the openness not to fear what may have seemed bizarre to many.

As Holmes's essays and novels demonstrate, he sensed and understood the emotional and intellectual changes catalyzing the Beats. *Go,* Holmes's first novel, captured the curious mixture of despair and new direction in the lives of writers like Ginsberg (David Stofsky in the novel) and Kerouac (Gene Pasternak). Later, in *The Horn,* Holmes tried new explorations into the world of jazz and hip values.

Holmes was the first person to make me see the extent of Kerouac's compassion and its paradoxical relation to his lonely isolation. Mellon's portrait in Holmes's library evokes his solid intellectuality and his love of literature. Kerouac, he told me, would come there to read his collection of Balzac. Several times in the mid-1960s, near the end of his life, Kerouac visited Holmes, and they would sit and drink for days. Kerouac was an indefatigable drinker at this point, Holmes explained, able to consume bottles of Courvoisier while spinning coiled monologues in torrential gusts: "He has talked out complete novels, with that utter recall, plus imaginative fire, that always astounds me."

＊　＊　＊　＊　＊　＊　＊　＊　＊　＊

The Frozen Fifties

From time to time there occurs some revolution, or sudden mutation of form and content in literature. Then, some way of writing which has been practised for a generation or more, is found by a few people to be out of date, and no longer to respond to contemporary modes of thought, feeling, and speech. A new kind of writing appears, to be greeted at first with disdain and derision; we hear that the tradition has been flouted, and that chaos has come. After a time it appears that the new way of writing is not destructive but re-creative. It is not that we have repudiated the past, as the obstinate enemies—and also the stupidest supporters—of any new movement like to believe, but that we have enlarged our conception of the past and in the light of what is new we see the past in a new pattern.

—**T. S. Eliot,** *"American Literature and Language"*

I The Syndrome of Shutdown

Those with a certain literary rectitude may find it odd to consider Eliot's remarks in the context of the Beat Generation. Kerouac, after all, in a manifesto he called "The Origins of Joy in Poetry," complained about Eliot's "dreary negative rules," about his "constipation" and the "emasculation of the pure masculine urge to freely sing."

While it is correct to assume that the openheartedness of many of the Beats was directly opposed to the calculated set of disguises and the elaborated "personae" informing Eliot's modernism, all writers have ancestors and spiritual fathers; they all exist in historical moments that can be measured and that motivate them to see their own past, as Eliot put it, "in a new pattern."

More than a half century ago, when the writers who would form the Beat Generation were establishing their first friendships in New York City, the United States was collectively about to win the largest-scale international conflict ever. Curiously, the individualism that had characterized the American way through the nineteenth century seemed threatened by new forces.

The historian Hannah Arendt, in the tradition of George Orwell's *1984*, declared that the postwar era was marked by the insidious emergence of faceless power, of "Rule by Nobody," as she put it. During the Truman administration, millions of Americans were investigated because of their imagined ideological sympathies. Allen Ginsberg called it the "Syndrome of Shutdown," the time of the closed society when the crucial decisions—shall we build thousands of nuclear devices, shall we inject nicotine into cigarettes?—would be made in secret.

Revisionist historians will argue that the Cold War and the threat of nuclear holocaust were primarily a means of maintaining and even accelerating an unprecedented rate of war production that had resolved all the economic issues perpetuating the Great Depression of the 1930s. From 1950 to 1953, defense spending tripled in the United States, and the country's major growth industry had become the production of sophisticated weapons systems. Disarmament meant recession, as the economy seemed inextricably tied to an armaments industry, and we began supplying the rest of the world with military hardware.

At the same time, military lobbyists and some politicians maintained that we lagged behind the Russians in attack capability. The Soviet invasion of Hungary in 1956, the erection of the Berlin Wall, and the launch of the Sputnik satellite in 1957, all seemed a confirmation of what the lobbyists had been saying.

The correlation between the defense budget and an unprecedented affluence was clear, though it would hardly have been politically correct to point it out in the 1950s. Affluence seems most compatible with denial, which by the 1950s had become endemic in the United States. This, of course, was the historical moment when big business merged with bureaucratic government, when the former heads of Procter & Gamble assumed control of the Food and Drug Administration.

The denial was also encouraged by a political climate of psychic terrorism, the so-called Red Menace dramatized by the trials of Alger Hiss and the Rosenbergs. As the novelist E. L. Doctorow noted in his brilliant fiction *The Book of Daniel*, based on the Rosenbergs, a spirit of fierce partisanship and recrimination dominated the postwar years, which he attributed "to the continuance beyond the end of the war of the war hysteria. Unfortunately, the necessary emotional fever for fighting a war cannot be turned off like a water faucet. Enemies must continue to be found. The mind and heart cannot be demobilized as quickly as the platoon. On the contrary, like a fiery furnace at white heat, it takes a considerable time to cool."

Actually, during the affluent fifties, the United States was being physically transformed. Seven million men had returned to make babies and build supermarkets, malls, and four-lane highways all over the country. Suddenly, radio had been replaced by television with its potential to condition us all into more efficient and insatiable consumers. Whereas our Puritan ancestors had taught Americans that borrowing money was ungodly, that excessive interest was usurious, postwar capitalism seized Keynes's notion of infinite credit for nations and applied it to the suburban family.

As a sign of the new comfort zones on the American horizon, the air conditioner could transform a fetid summer afternoon and remove the sweat from a man's brow. This innovation was reflected in the rapid development of Arizona and the Southwest, just as it became the title of Henry Miller's jeremiad *The Air-Conditioned Nightmare,* a book denouncing the changes Miller saw on his return to the United States during the war years after a decade of expatriation.

For most, the new technology was a convenient distraction from any political costs to freedom in the United States. The Cold War hysteria was accelerated by Senator Joseph McCarthy's allegations of traitors in the State Department, and the House Un-American Activities Committee witch-hunts in academia and Hollywood.

The gossip columnist Hedda Hopper's remark that those suspected of disloyalty were best interned in concentration camps is a touchstone of the irresponsible dimensions of political rage at that time. Soon the enormous inquisitional terror of a federal HUAC was replicated state by state by similar committees intent on declaring what it meant to be an American.

The right-wing persecution was not entirely without precedent or basis. The first Red Scare had occurred during the First World War, when the Russian Bolsheviks withdrew from the battlefield and were seen as deserting the Allied cause. In the United States, as Warren Beatty's film *Reds* suggests, there was considerable fear that workers and their unions would be organized by Communists loyal only to Moscow.

This same fear was prevalent after the Second World War. The war had brought Americans together and made them suspicious of questioning and dissent. Some of McCarthy's victims were involved in espionage, some had been active in left-wing causes, some did have associations with Communists. The American Communist Party was dependent on Soviet financing, which meant Soviet control. Party members, who were after all members of a secret society, accepted the dogma of the Party line. I remember students at CCNY in the late 1950s who naively still revered Stalin and Mao as gods who could not fail and refused to admit that these men had butchered and sacrificed millions of their own countrymen for the sake of expedience.

The repercussions of the Red Scare were enormous, from the suicide of Harvard scholar F. O. Matthiesson—author of *American Renaissance,* the classic study of American transcendentalism—to the dismissal of sixty professors at the University of California at Berkeley in 1951 for refusing to sign loyalty oaths. There are thousands of other examples. The poet Gary Snyder, a young man working for the U.S. Forest Service early in the 1950s, was discharged as a security risk—a case of the poet preaching to the trees?—because of radical associations as an undergraduate at Reed College. Allen Ginsberg's companion Peter Orlovsky was reading a book by psychiatrist Erich Fromm at boot camp in West Virginia in 1953, which caused an army lieutenant to call him a Communist. Orlovsky was transferred to a San Francisco hospital, where he completed his military service as a medic.

The magazine *Red Channels* caused a blacklisting of intellectuals who may have signed a petition two decades earlier, of artists and writers with leftist or progressive perspectives. The FBI used illegal wiretaps and created the Security Index, a list of millions of citizens who might require detention in the event of national emergency. These attempts to poison the atmosphere with fear and to enforce conformity at all costs succeeded in debilitating and marginalizing all progressive programs from disarmament to civil rights.

One register of the psychic contamination during the Korean War period in the early 1950s was recalled by the poet Michael McClure in his book *Scratching the Beat Surface:*

> My self-image in those years was of finding myself—young, high, a little crazed, needing a haircut, in an elevator with burly, crew-cutted, square-jawed eminences staring at me like I

was misplaced cannon fodder. We hated the war and the inhumanity and the coldness. The country had the feeling of martial law. An undeclared military state had leapt out of Daddy Warbucks' tanks and sprawled over the landscape. As artists we were oppressed.

One major symptom of the repression was a culture of informing—actually what the Communists had effected in postwar China and Russia—so at Harvard one Henry Kissinger, a teaching fellow in the early 1950s, was accused of opening his fellow students' mail and passing some of it to the FBI. Ronald Reagan, president of the Screen Actors Guild, had been an FBI informant since the early 1940s.

The American Puritans had imagined pagan frolics in the woods and guilt by association with Satan. The new informers intoned the names of the guilty before secret committees. Some of the informers, like the failed novelist Whittaker Chambers, were drunkards with powerful imaginations and the novelistic ability to spin a good story. Others were seeking advancement. Informers were rewarded in many ways, but the most shocking aspect of the matter is that J. Edgar Hoover, director of the FBI, insisted that the informant's identity had to be shielded. It was enough to be named to be considered guilty, and this represented a profound reversal of what had been considered an essential American liberty.

The paternal, benevolently benign presence overseeing the political repression of the 1950s was Dwight D. Eisenhower, the Supreme Allied Commander during the Second World War, and a representative figure who helps explain his era. His radiant grin seemed derived from a Grant Wood painting or a Sherwood Anderson story. In her novel *The Bell Jar*, the poet Sylvia Plath aggressively compared Eisenhower's bald head and blank stare to a "foetus in a bottle," but her harsh image underestimated the attraction of his placating but firm charm. Ike's rounded face suggested a placid contentment and a beguiling innocence, a heartland look Americans associated with an old-fashioned optimism and courage.

As the most popular American of his time, Eisenhower could be used by fund-raisers, whether for Columbia University, which was his apprenticeship in civilian administration, or the Republican Party. He delegated his authority freely, to men like the Dulles brothers in matters of foreign policy and espionage, and to Charles Wilson, his Secretary of Defense, who insisted that whatever was good for General Motors was good for the country. That sentiment became the unspoken ideology of the fifties, and the utility of corporate profits the ultimate value. Only a very select group of artists and intellectuals could see that to succeed, the mercantile mind—what Ginsberg called "Moloch"—would even sacrifice the environment for the sake of the profit motive. Of course, such rapacity was not traditionally associated with democratic governance, which was supposed to exist for the good of the people.

Although Eisenhower was an uninspiring speaker, he became an icon of confident victory in a new kind of war. Eisenhower was the presiding figure during the 1950s, a moment when notions of personal responsibility were being subsumed by the values caused by an unprecedentedly sophisticated technology and corporate largeness, when the future was being mortgaged to the Pentagon, when the industrial oligarchy that Eisenhower warned us of in his farewell address was perpetuating the power of the police state.

II   The Control State

I think this fear of arbitrary authority relates to an important part of the Beats' prophecy. In the preface to Barry Miles's 1986 edition of the facsimile *Howl*, Allen Ginsberg remarks that in writing the poem "I was curious to leave behind after my generation an emotional time bomb that would continue exploding in U.S. consciousness in case our military-industrial-nationalist complex solidified into a repressive police bureaucracy." This was a shared, central Beat sentiment.

For example, in one of the rare political moments in *On the Road*, Sal Paradise, Dean Moriarty, and a few friends arrive in Washington, D.C., on the day of Truman's inauguration for his second term. Driving down

Pennsylvania Avenue, Kerouac observed that "great displays of war might" lined the street: "B-29's, PT boats, all kinds of war material that looked murderous in the snowy grass."

In the next scene, after being stopped for speeding and harassed by police because of their appearance, Kerouac observed, "The American police are involved in psychological warfare against those Americans who don't frighten them with imposing papers and threats. It's a Victorian police force; it peers out of musty windows and wants to inquire about everything, and can make crimes if the crimes don't exist to its satisfaction."

One such "criminal" was William S. Burroughs, who in 1947 was growing marijuana secreted between rows of alfalfa on his farm in New Waverly, Texas. He was trying to grow opium, which doesn't grow north of the Rio Grande, but didn't he anticipate a multibillion-dollar business that the government ultimately could not control? Control, of course, is very much to the point: *"You see, control,"* Burroughs tells us in italics in *Naked Lunch,* *"can never be a means to any practical end. . . . It can never be a means to anything but more control. . . . Like junk . . . "*

In Texas, Burroughs observed how the agricultural bureaucracy conspired to provide migrant labor for the big farmers at peon's wages. Actually, the federal bureaucracy tripled under Truman, and that had to trouble so arch an individualist as Burroughs, who, when I interviewed him in 1974, even denied belonging to the Beat movement. Burroughs would later relentlessly parody bureaucrats and authority figures in *Naked Lunch,* his nightmarish vision of a society in a state of entropy that develops a perspective so nihilistic as to believe in nothing, certainly not in any organized system.

Burroughs's discontinuity—his microcosmic focus on what frequently appear to be unrelatable experiences—is part of a similar attempt to deny the organic unities of nineteenth-century structure in poetry and fiction. Burroughs's use of the "cut-up" method—an arbitrary juxtaposition of randomly selected words and phrases—is part of an attempt to restructure the grammar of perception; the new linguistic order that Burroughs invents initiates the Beats' assault on the conditioning influences of language.

Burroughs takes the motif of the Unreal City from *The Waste Land*

and compounds it with a nauseating imagery of hideous physical disinte-gration and degradation that promises a state of future plague. His hanged-men episodes in *Naked Lunch* are grotesque parodies of the talis-manic material Eliot himself parodied with the grail legend in *The Waste Land*.

Burroughs presents these horrors with an unsettling calm, a cold earnestness reminiscent of Swift, a view of the psychological transforma-tions latent in fantasy close to Kafka. His view of man as helpless victim reminds us of Sartre, Beckett, and Genet. Entering the absolute nadir of existence, Burroughs's fiction defines a purgatory of endless suffering—Beat in the sense of beaten, oppressed, and dehumanized.

If there is a political center in *Naked Lunch*, it is the equation of can-cer and bureaucracy:

> The end result of complete cellular representation is cancer. Democracy is cancerous, and bureaus are its cancer. A bureau takes root anywhere in the state, turns malignant like the Nar-cotic Bureau, and grows and grows, always reproducing more of its own kind, until it chokes the host if not controlled or excised. Bureaus cannot live without a host, being true parasitic organ-isms. (A cooperative on the other hand *can* live without the state. That is the road to follow. The building up of independent units to meet needs of the people who participate in the func-tioning of the unit. A bureau operates on opposite principle of *inventing* needs to justify its existence.) Bureaucracy is wrong as a cancer, a turning away from the human evolutionary direc-tion of infinite potentials and differentiation and independent spontaneous action, to the complete parasitism of a virus.

William Burroughs's identification of bureaucracy as the cancer in democracy may seem offensive, though it is characteristic of the apocalyp-tic urgency of the Beats. I have taught the novel to undergraduates for two decades, and this is a book that more profoundly than any other violates the nerve endings and offends.

Of course, what was most threatening about *Naked Lunch* from the establishment's point of view was not its predictive warning of the drug plague that would sap the support systems of Western civilization but its detailed, "factualist" accounting of bizarre sexual rituals, the cannibalistic mutilations and orgasmic death hangings that seem related, however loosely, to the Mayan practices that fascinated Burroughs when he studied at Mexico City College in the early 1950s.

Burroughs described the factualist style in a letter to Ginsberg dated November 9, 1948: "All arguments, all nonsensical considerations as to what people 'should do' are irrelevant. Ultimately, there is only fact on all levels, and the more one argues, verbalizes, moralizes, the less he will see and feel of fact." For Burroughs, "factualism" meant that the writer had to suspend any moral evaluation, which since Fielding and the first stirrings of the novel as a form had been an obligatory priority.

It is difficult for us now to imagine the radical depth of Burroughs's suspension of moral judgment. The 1950s were an era when any public discussion of sexual matters in the United States was taboo, when masturbation was seen as a cause of insanity and premarital sex as immoral, when half of American women were married by the age of nineteen, oral sex was considered sheer perversion, and adultery and homosexuality were regarded as criminal acts. In 1950, a group of Republican senators accused the Truman administration of being rife with homosexuals, and one of President Eisenhower's first executive orders made homosexuality grounds for disbarment from any form of federal employment.

So lines like "Gentle reader, we see God through our assholes in the flash bulb of orgasm"—which Burroughs wrote in Tangier in the mid-1950s—were considered as intolerable (certainly in Boston, at least, where the courts had to decide whether the book could be sold) as the fact that Dr. Alfred Kinsey, an obscure investigator of gall wasps from Indiana University, had amassed some eighteen thousand sexual case histories, many in the Times Square area and three of them with Burroughs, Ginsberg, and Kerouac.

I see Kinsey's sexual explorations as a parallel to Freud's curiosities about the mind, although when *Sexual Behavior in the Human Male* appeared in 1948 and the subsequent report on women in 1953, these studies were viciously attacked by psychiatrists and psychoanalysts for reporting data rather than making judgments. In other words, psychiatists, like the Victorian novelists of an earlier era, were expected to enforce social controls, to condemn, vilify, or declare medically abnormal what the power elite could not publicly condone.

Incidentally, many of these same psychiatrists vigorously proposed electroshock therapy for depression even though it effectively erased memory and was so crudely barbarous as a technique patients had to be strapped down during convulsions. After shock treatments the patient— take, for example, Carl Solomon, to whom *Howl* is dedicated—was placed on a permanent lifetime diet (or is the word "addiction"?) to drugs like Thorazine, drugs that lead us to Prozac or Huxley's prediction of the soma that would control us all.

III   Derelicts

Each of the Beats turned to writing because of a psychic wound: Burroughs had his childhood nightmares and the murder of his wife, Kerouac was four when his older brother Gerard died of rheumatic fever, Ginsberg suffered with his troubled mother, Naomi.

It is illuminating, in this connection, to note that the catalyst figures for each of the Beats—Solomon for Ginsberg, Huncke for Burroughs, and Neal Cassady for Kerouac—were all wounded figures as well, perennial outsiders who had enormous difficulty living within what they called "the system." Solomon spent eight years in mental hospitals, and ended his life working as a messenger. Like Huncke and Cassady, he was a talker, and he told me he had talked his way into the bin, which made him an American "untouchable." Both Huncke and Cassady were untouchables as well because they had been to prison for theft, although Cassady's incarceration was in a reform school for having stolen the Denver district attorney's car on a dare. All three relied on drugs, Solomon on Thorazine, Cassady on amphetamines and marijuana—he was known as the Johnny Appleseed of the West Coast—and Huncke on an entire pharmacology of opiates.

But even more important than their outlaw status was the fact that each aspired to write, Solomon with his pithy essays, Huncke with his stories of circus life and the hustler's road, Cassady with the awkward story of his childhood on the Denver bowery. While these men were sympathetically accepted as "dumbsaints," to use Kerouac's term—and the crucial point of the entire Beat enterprise was exactly this sympathetic encouragement—they were shunned by the rest of the world as crazy deviants or con men.

No wonder the postwar years seemed to artists to be an imperiled period of profound powerlessness. This was true on a general scale—not just true of the writers I am discussing here. The novelist William Styron claimed his generation had been "cut to pieces" by the trauma of the war and the "almost unimaginable presence of the bomb." In *The Prisoner of Sex*, Norman Mailer wondered how he survived those years without losing his mind. The Abstract Expressionist painter Adolph Gottlieb remembered painting with "a feeling of absolute desperation." His generation "felt like derelicts," Gottlieb maintained. "Everything felt hopeless and we had nothing to lose."

Gottlieb's word "derelict" is on the same wavelength as Herbert Huncke's "beat," the term that led Jack Kerouac to name a generation. Jack Kerouac defined "beat" as the state of a spirit that had been so defeated, so beaten down by experience, that the writer could honestly confess his deepest, most personal feelings without inhibition or shame because there was nothing to lose.

Beat begins with a sense of cultural displacement and disaffiliation, a distrust of official "truth," an awareness that things are often not what they seem to be, which is a fundamental point of departure for writers. Kerouac would later extend his definition by relating Beat to beatitude, a state of bliss achieved through jazz, sex, meditation, writing, or any other intense experience in which the sense of self is obliterated. The object was to open the individual through the doors of feeling, to leave him vulnerable, sympathetic, and receptive.

I have too much respect for Kerouac's fiction to suggest that it was self-consciously philosophical or in any sense a programmatic exposition. But the famous characters in *On the Road*, with their sometimes frenetic searches for the next visionary epiphany, their mad, ecstatic conversations, and their cross-country journeys, are in flight from an America they found too coldhearted—so they found it difficult to breathe in an atmosphere of envy, fear, competition, and suspicion. At the same time—forming a central tension in the novel—it is a flight in pursuit of an American warmth for which Kerouac yearned and which suffused his fiction, a quality that made some of his critics condemn him for sentimentality.

The reviewers misread the novel almost without exception, finding it incoherent, unstructured, unsound as art, and unhappy as prophecy. Instead of seeing Dean Moriarty as a genuine picaresque center, and thereby a source of unity in a novel about turbulence, the reviewers attacked the sensibility of nihilism.

It is, perhaps, easier to see Dean today as a remarkable fusion of desperation and joy, as the "ragged and ecstatic joy of pure being," to borrow Kerouac's description, an utterly rootless individual who careens from coast to coast on sudden impulse, a man whose incredible energy makes a mockery of the false idol of security.

Dean is drawn in the tradition of Huckleberry Finn but is untainted by Miss Watson's puritanism; as a result he is without guile or guilt. The sign of Dean's freedom is his infectious laughter, a token of spirit representing a life force. Merely to laugh at the world, like the existentialist ability to say no, becomes a valuable source of inspiration for Kerouac. Dean has been in jail and reads Proust; but his defining quality is speed—in conversation, in a car, in his lifestyle.

Kerouac, depicting Dean as a function of speed, has saliently tapped the distinguishing strain of American life in the second half of the twentieth century. This speed is reflected in an extraordinary hyperactivity that determines the atmosphere of the novel: "the only people for me are the mad ones, the ones who are mad to live, mad to talk, mad to be saved, desirous of everything at the same time, the ones who never yawn or say a commonplace thing but burn, burn, burn like fabulous yellow roman candles exploding like spiders across the stars."

Kerouac himself, through the figure of his narrator, Sal Paradise, tried to offer a check on Dean's exuberant anarchism; indeed, one of the bases for scenic organization in the novel is the way in which other characters find fault with Dean. And Sal is inevitably drained by the momentum of experience, always aware of growing older and saddened by this; like Kerouac, he is an outsider, an imperfect man in an alien world, brooding, lonely, seized by moments of self-hatred. The refrain in *On the Road* of "everything is collapsing" is a reminder of the effects of disorder, of Kerouac's own vision of uncontained release, on himself. Clearly, the endless celebrations, the pell-mell rushing from one scene to the next, create a hysteria that makes Sal want to withdraw from the world.

IV   The Great Divide

Early in the 1950s, as a student in the New York City public schools, I experienced the kind of endemic powerlessness in the face of Big Government that provoked the Beats, and that in a full swing of the historical pendulum caused the sustained challenge to authority of the 1960s. I refer to the humiliations of what were called Civil Defense drills, when sirens would suddenly wail and we would all cower under our tiny desks in tense, almost fetal anticipation, or file into dark basement shelters that even we knew offered no protection, no relief for the dread that was being fostered in us.

Nelson Rockefeller, a scion of Standard Oil who didn't need more income, and governor of New York State, had defended the importance of such drills and started a company for the fabrication of shelters. In New York State, participation in Civil Defense drills was mandatory.

When Judith Malina of The Living Theatre joined Dorothy Day of the Catholic Worker movement to defy mandatory compliance, in June of 1955 in the park outside New York's City Hall, Malina was remanded to Bellevue by a judge who decided such protest was a sign of insanity. In elementary and junior high school, where we began our day by pledging allegiance, none of us were free enough to scream out that these drills were a farce. Later, these drills seemed paradigmatic, semaphores for the frozen fifties and its emphasis on conformity at all costs.

Preposterously, in 1954, *Walden* had been removed from all United States Information Agency libraries because of its alleged "socialism." In October of that year, the postmaster of Los Angeles refused to deliver a little magazine called *One,* the first consequential gay magazine, on the grounds of obscenity. We must remember that in 1956, *Howl* would be confiscated by the San Francisco customs police on the same grounds, and that the right to publish *Naked Lunch* would have to be established in the courts.

The world was quite different then. In 1955, interracial marriage was still banned in thirty states, and the Democratic Party ballot in Alabama was headed by the slogan "White Supremacy." The struggle for civil rights was often linked to subversion, seen as part of a left-wing attempt to weaken the social fabric. When the Supreme Court in its historic *Brown* decision voted to end segregation, Senator Sam Eastland of Mississippi declared the judges to be brainwashed victims of a Communist plot.

There were subtle sounds of change evident in the mid-fifties. In California, the Pacifica Foundation started broadcasting on radio station KPFA. In New York, critic Irving Howe began *Dissent* and Norman Mailer helped found the *Village Voice* in 1955. A disc jockey symbolically named Allan Freed changed the format of his program from rhythm and blues to rock and roll, playing Chuck Berry, Fats Domino, Bo Diddley, Little Richard, and then Elvis Presley.

This great divide was the beginning of the culture wars. An early sally was provided by Frank Sinatra, testifying before a congressional committee. In a spirit of malicious self-interest, he claimed that rock music "was the most brutal, ugly, desperate, vicious form of expression it has been my misfortune to hear" and that "by means of its almost imbecilic reiterations and sly, lewd, and in plain fact dirty lyrics, manages to be the martial music of every sideburned delinquent on the face of the earth."

V An Emotional Time Bomb

When I began college in 1957, there was already the shared sense that the cultural climate could change if enough of us resisted. That was a seething and fertile period for New York City, and I shared in it, attending avant-garde concerts at Columbia University's McMillan Theater, some of the Abstract Expressionist shows, and almost all of the plays being done by The Living Theatre at its Fourteenth Street location.

Part of the liberating headiness of that moment—an antidote to the poisonous contaminations of the Cold War—was the aesthetic thunderbolt of works like *Howl, On the Road,* and *Naked Lunch,* all of which I read as an undergraduate. These works were signifiers of a new consciousness, although it would take a few decades for that to be appreciated on a broad cultural level.

In Pound's tradition of "Make It New," each of these books proposed something fundamentally new about form and perspective. In *Howl,* the first of these works to appear, the dithyrambic rhythm and length of Ginsberg's line, the surging locomotion and momentum of the strophes, were an attempt to hypnotize the reader into a realization of what was crippling and wrong about America. *Howl* defined a new sensibility in its rush of raw feeling, and its hyperbole was a way to rouse what Robert Lowell had called the tranquilized fifties. The rhapsodic rant of the "Holy! Holy!" near the end of the poem was a Whitmanesque cry of identification with human suffering.

The goal of complete self-revelation, of nakedness, as Ginsberg put it, was in *Howl* based on a fusion of bohemianism, psychoanalytic probing, and Dadaist fantasy that dragged the self through the slime of degradation to the sublime of exaltation. While the idea of self is a Beat focal point, it represents only a beginning, an involvement to be transcended. The movement in Ginsberg's poetry is from an intense assertion of personal identity to a merger with larger forces in the universe. The ensuing tension between the proclamation of self—evident in a poem like "America"—and an insistence upon man's eternal place in time creates a central opposition in Ginsberg's poetry.

Believing that consciousness is infinite, and that modern man has been taught to suppress much of his potential awareness, Ginsberg attempted to exorcise the shame, guilt, and fear that he saw as barriers to self-realization and total being. Ginsberg's work, generally, is an out-growth of the tradition begun by Blake and Coleridge: an effort to search for the source of dream, to release the unconscious in its pure state (avoid-ing literary simulation), to free the restraints on imagination so as to feel the potency and power of the visionary impulse.

Ginsberg saw his poetry as transmitting a sacred trust in human potentials, and he spoke in a *Paris Review* interview of how his mystical encounter with Blake in 1948 revealed the nature and direction of his own search as a poet. Ginsberg, then living in New York's East Harlem, sud-denly heard a voice reciting Blake's "Ah! Sun-flower" and "The Sick Rose." The resulting feeling of lightness, awe, and wonder catalyzed him as a poet, making him see that his role would be to widen the area of con-sciousness, to open the doors of perception, to transmit messages through time that could reach the enlightened and receptive.

Ginsberg's poetry is characteristic of the Beat desire *to be*, affirming existence as a positive value in a time of apathy. The quest for experience is as obsessive and all-consuming in "Howl" as in *On the Road*. Whether these experiences are destructive or not is of less importance than the fact of contact, of the kind of experience that allows an individual to discover his own vulnerability, his humanness, without cowering.

As Gary Snyder has argued in his essay "Why Tribe," to follow the grain of natural being "it is necessary to look exhaustively into the nega-tive and demonic powers of the Unconscious, and by recognizing these powers—symbolically acting them out—one releases himself from these forces." This statement points to the shamanistic implications of Beat lit-erature; "Howl," like *Naked Lunch*, is an attempt to exorcise through release. While Burroughs's novel futuristically projects into fantasy, "Howl" naturalistically records the suffering and magnanimity of a hipster avant-garde, a group that refuses to accept standard American values and materialism as permanent.

The experiences in "Howl," certainly in the opening part of the poem, are hysterically excessive and frantically active. It is the sheer momentum of nightmare that unifies these accounts of jumping off bridges, of slashing wrists, of ecstatic copulations, of purgatorial subway rides and longer journeys, a momentum rendered by the propelling, torrential quality of Ginsberg's long line, a cumulative rhythm, dependant on parallelism and the repetition of initial sounds that is biblical in origin.

Ginsberg's poetry ranges in tone from joy to utter despair, soaring and plunging from one line to the next, confident, paranoid, always seeking ways to awaken us in the somnambulism of our denial, to regain the ability to *feel* in numbing times, always insisting on a social vision that stresses transcendence and the need for spirit in the face of a materialistic culture.

VI Wildfire

These three writers were not simply arguing rebellion. As Allen Ginsberg remarked in a letter to his father dated November 30, 1957, rebellion was a minor element:

> What we are saying is that these values are not really standard or permanent, and we are in a sense I think ahead of the times. . . . When you have a whole economy involved in some version of moneymaking—this just is no standard of values. That it seems to offer a temporary security may be enough to keep people slaving for it. But meanwhile it destroys real value. And it ultimately breaks down. Whitman long ago complained that unless the material power of America was leavened by some kind of spiritual infusion we would wind up among the

"fabled damned." It seems we're approaching that state as far as I can see. Only way out is individuals taking responsibility and saying what they actually feel—which is an enormous human achievement in any society. That's just what we as a group have been trying to do. To class that as some form of "rebellion" in the kind of college-bred social worker doubletalk . . . misses the huge awful point.

And just as the Beat Generation was not simply about rebellion, it was not exclusively about the work of Ginsberg, Kerouac, and Burroughs. A generational recognition spreads like wildfire, and in this case it included at least a hundred other writers such as Gary Snyder, Lawrence Ferlinghetti, Gregory Corso, and Michael McClure, and it continued into a succeeding generation.

The extent to which the Beat Generation existed on a national level in the 1950s, also, has not been fully appreciated, and outposts existed in cities like Chicago with the literary magazine *Big Table,* and in Kansas City and New Orleans.

The best-documented instance of the immediate flowering of Beat culture is in the San Francisco Bay area. Kerouac acknowledged in *Desolation Angels* that San Francisco "tugged at your heart" like New York City, and both places—promontories into the sea, really—represented traditional escapes from Main Street, U.S.A.

The poet Philip Lamantia, whose family emigrated to San Francisco from Italy at the beginning of the twentieth century, has remarked that after World War II, the North Beach area was buoyed by a euphoric energy as it filled with conscientious objectors, anarchists, and "poet-orientalist-surrealist-majic-jazzed-out-alchemy heads." These newcomers were regarded with suspicion by the local Italians, who as a group were slow to assimilate and would not tolerate demonstrations of sexual freedom or racial mixing on the street.

A key figure was Kenneth Rexroth, the paterfamilias of the West Coast Beats, who began poetry readings with jazz musicians in the Fillmore area. Rexroth had the idea for the famous Six Gallery reading where Ginsberg first read "Howl," which became the defining moment of what was called the San Francisco Renaissance.

Rexroth had organized the Libertarian Circle, an anarchist discussion group that held weekly meetings, evolving into a sort of bohemian salon. The conversations continued during the week at cafés with a distinctly European flavor—like the intellectual hangout Vesuvio's; the Cellar; the Black Cat Café; the Co-Existence Bagel Shop, where Richard Brautigan would read; and the Hungry i (for "id"), where comedians like Woody Allen, Mort Sahl, Bill Cosby, Mike Nichols, and Elaine May performed, and where Lenny Bruce was arrested.

The poets whose voices animated this floating salon attended Ruth Witt-Diamant's poetry series at San Francisco State (Ginsberg met McClure at Auden's reading in 1954), and some of them studied with Robert Duncan. They started a number of small magazines that continued the energy. *Circle Magazine* in Berkeley published Anaïs Nin and Henry Miller (then living a few hundred miles to the south in Big Sur). Some of these magazines were very fluid: *Inferno* became *Ark*, which became *Ark Moby* when McClure edited it in 1956. The editorship of a mimeographed publication called *Beatitude* was passed from poet to poet (although it was mostly run by Bob Kaufman), prompting Lawrence Ferlinghetti to call it a "floating crap-game," even though it was a successful demonstration of anarchism.

Another crucial part of this literary scene was the magazine *City Lights,* named, after Chaplin's film, by Peter Martin, who taught at San Francisco State and who was the son of an assassinated Italian anarchist named Carlo Fresca. In 1953, Ferlinghetti joined Martin to form the first paperback bookstore in America and a publishing company, both called City Lights, to disseminate anarchist and Beat writing.

Some of the Beats, or their cousins, are still relatively unknown, like Judith Malina and Julian Beck, who formed The Living Theatre, the most radical, dynamic theatrical group of our time. Writing my history of The Living Theatre, which Grove Press published in 1995, I read Julian's journal accounts of meeting Jack Kerouac at Horace Mann in 1939, and of reading "Howl" to Judith when that great poem first appeared in 1956. I told the story of The Living Theatre, incarnate heroes or martyrs of Beat underground culture, only quite recently, and my point here is that the history of the Beat movement has only begun to be transcribed. The huge

Whitney Museum 1995 exhibit "Beat Culture and the New America," the show of Burroughs's paintings and collages at the Los Angeles County Museum of Art in 1996, the Viking Press publication of Burroughs's letters in 1993, Kerouac's letters in 1995, and *Some of the Dharma* in 1997, and William Morrow's publication of *The Herbert Huncke Reader* in 1997 are clear signs of mounting interest in the Beat legacy.

William Burroughs told me in 1972 that the Beats were primarily a cultural rather than a literary force, and I argued then, as I do now, that any genuine literature ultimately helps to shape the culture and gives it some of its aspiration. The Beats may be one trigger for the sixties, but I think their influence goes far beyond that decade. The Beat message will become even more prominent in the twenty-first century as the powers assumed by political states are concentrated, as such threats as biological warfare encourage the employment of technological means to control populations, as bureaucracy compromises and corrodes the concept of human rights everywhere.

< < < < < O > > > > > > > > > > > >

Herbert Huncke, Boulder, Colorado, 1982.

Herbert Huncke, the incarnate underground man, is one of the original members of the Beat Generation. Celebrated as Elmo Hassel in Kerouac's *On the Road,* as Huck in *Visions of Cody,* and as Herman in Burroughs's *Junky,* Huncke participated in the quest for forbidden experience that brought the Beats together in New York City at the end of the Second World War.

Indeed, although he would modestly demur, Huncke introduced Burroughs, Kerouac, and Ginsberg to morphine and to criminal aspects of life of which they were previously unaware, and which profoundly affected both the character and content of their writing.

Huncke was a Beat code figure: hitchhiking around America as a teenage runaway, shipping out on freighters, the Times Square hustle, and the hipster scene constituted his education. But what proved most irresistible for the Beats about Huncke was his ability as a raconteur. His voice expressed the raw sociology of literature, unaffected by ego, unaffiliated with any recognizable element of society. He was an untouchable of the drug underclass afflicted with the resonance of his own pain, and he spoke with the unadorned directness of the man on the next barstool.

Huncke wrote naturalistic stories about his experiences on the road all of his life, and some of them appeared in appropriately fugitive forums. Ironically, perhaps, his work has recently been presented by William Morrow to a more mainstream audience in *The Herbert Huncke Reader.*

I met Huncke in the spring of 1973. He had been jailed many times, so he was cautious, though he very much wanted his story to surface. I was certainly curious, though unsettled when I saw the scar tissue that covered the veins on his arms and the black circles around his eyes. He told me how he had met Dr. Alfred Kinsey in Times Square after the war when the researcher was conducting his interviews on the sexual habits of the American male. Huncke became one of his recruiters; he would find subjects for a fee.

I saw Herbert many times over the next quarter century, and was consistently impressed by a sweetness that dominated even his chronic complaints. Mellon's photograph captures a preening, almost dandy side that contradicts Huncke's more raffish popular image, the look of vacancy that Burroughs described in *Junky.*

Huncke was notorious for requesting small loans that he could never hope to repay. Once he asked me to buy him a drink at the Lion's Head in Sheridan Square, and then nervously asked for a twenty. Rejection had been such an important element in his life, but also, as only the hipster understands, so had the propriety of doing things in the right way. I did not hesitate—it was a small price for what he had given to me.

Burroughs and Huncke, Boulder, 1982.

Burroughs met Huncke early in 1945 in a railroad apartment on Henry Street on the Lower East Side. As part of a mysterious affinity with an underworld he sought to explore, Burroughs had obtained a sawed-off submachine gun and a supply of morphine syrettes, part of the first-aid kits of soldiers on the frontline during the war.

The tenement apartment looked like an exotic drug den, and Burroughs surmised he was in the right place. Its walls had been painted black, the ceilings were red, and around a light fixture in the living room was an arrangement of squares and triangles in different colors that would compound the effects of any drug. It made an impression on him he would later reflect in *Junky*.

Huncke told me his first impression of Burroughs was that he was "heat": in a three-piece suit, a Chesterfield overcoat he would not remove, and a snap-brim fedora, he resembled a stockbroker.

"Who is this guy?" he asked a friend in the apartment. "He looks like trouble."

Allen Ginsberg and William Burroughs, Boulder, 1982.

Kerouac named his generation and was its spokesman, but Ginsberg was its inveterate organizer, its most committed missionary.

As soon as Ginsberg was elected to the National Institute of Arts and Letters in 1973 he began a decade of lobbying on Burroughs's behalf. Although Burroughs had admirers in the institute, writers like Christopher Isherwood and Mary McCarthy, there was a genteel opposition led by the venerable Glenway Wescott, a mannered Jamesian, who objected to the scatological elements of Burroughs's fiction.

The key figure in Burroughs's election was Leon Edel, Henry James's biographer. Ginsberg approached Edel in 1981, and Edel agreed to second the nomination even though he admitted to having read Burroughs only in "bits and pieces."

Leon Edel was my mentor. He had chosen me to act as his assistant, ironically just as a skirt-chaser in the English department at NYU had denied my application to teach freshmen. Edel directed my doctoral thesis on James, and he was the first person to whom I sent the published version of *Naked Angels*. That was virtually his introduction to the Beats, and he applauded it, calling it a "definitive history." Always a shrewd politician of the word, Allen knew this and acted accordingly.

After his induction to the institute in 1983, Burroughs was asked by his biographer Ted Morgan how it felt to be saluted by a company that included Saul Bellow, John Updike, and Arthur Miller. Burroughs replied: "Twenty years ago, they were saying I belonged in jail. Now they're saying I don't belong in their club. I didn't listen to them then, and I don't listen to them now."

David Amram at piano with film crew,
Boulder, 1982.

A gifted and versatile musician who performed with Dizzy Gillespie, Thelonius Monk, and Charlie Mingus, David Amram was a close friend of Jack Kerouac's. In 1957, as one of the initial touchstones of the jazz-poetry movement, he played accompaniment as Kerouac rapped, improvised, and recited haiku and poems at the Brata Art Gallery on East Tenth Street or the Circle in the Square Theatre in Greenwich Village.

I am seated at David Amram's feet with the film crew that shot *Kerouac: The Movie*. John Antonelli, a young man from Lowell, Massachusetts, Kerouac's hometown, had asked me to write a screenplay for a film on Kerouac. The fact that Antonelli was a Lowell native and tremendously eager convinced me to begin an apprenticeship in a new medium.

The photograph was taken at the Naropa Institute, the first Buddhist university in the United States. Naropa had been founded by Chogyam Trungpa Rinpoche, a reincarnated lama, a poet, a calligrapher, and a master of the Kagyu or "crazy wisdom" school of Tibetan Buddhism. Serendipitously, he met Ginsberg on the street in the East Village in 1970 when his assistant recognized the poet. In 1974, with Anne Waldman, Ginsberg started the Jack Kerouac School of Disembodied Poetics at Naropa as a gathering place where poets, students, scholars, and artists could meet and exchange energies.

In 1982, Naropa sponsored a celebration of the twenty-fifth anniversary of the publication of *On the Road,* a giant Beat assembling with literary panels and parties. Ferlinghetti, John Clellon Holmes, McClure, Ginsberg, and others read. An art show featured Jack Kerouac's paintings, Burroughs's collages, and Robert LaVigne's painting of Peter Orlovsky. Allen Ginsberg, Elsa Dorfman, and Mellon displayed some of their photographs of the Beats.

David Amram is still dedicated to Kerouac's memory. In 1997, I spoke on Ezra Pound at a festival in Goes, Holland, that included more musicians than literary types, and David was there.

He was going to play his musical arrangement of Kerouac's poem "Pull My Daisy" on the bells of the old Dutch church in the center of the circular town, and he asked me to accompany him. We carried a variety of instruments that he needed for a performance later that evening up four twisted flights of uneven stone steps. Finally, there was a double flight of wooden steps with no railing going straight up to the bell tower.

The view of Goes and the surrounding countryside was quaint and pastoral. I found it amusing that the melody for this slightly pornographic little poem would be heard on Puritan bells. Afterward, we descended carrying flutes and drums. A fountain of exuberant energy, David continued one of his interminable, often hilarious raps, reminiscing about the Kerouac he knew in the 1950s.

John Tytell and Robert Creeley, Boulder, 1982.

The "No Ideas but in Things" T-shirt—poet William Carlos Williams's credo—was a present from my creative writing students. It was appropriate for Creeley, who, like Ginsberg and Kerouac, descends in part from William Carlos Williams. When Ginsberg completed his undergraduate study at Columbia, Kerouac advised him to return to Paterson, New Jersey, his hometown, to meet Williams, who was a pediatrician there, and to learn from his diction, his precision and suppleness.

Creeley's sly and sinuous verse line owes much to Williams as well. In the spring of 1956, at the height of the San Francisco Renaissance, Creeley joined Ginsberg and Kerouac on the West Coast. All three young writers were students of Williams's notion that the poem was revealed to the poet through the process of writing—Kerouac's spontaneity—as opposed to a more old-fashioned strategy depending on preconceived and predetermined effects.

Creeley told me that Ginsberg revealed the value of using his own emotional life as subject matter and that Kerouac encouraged him to pursue a more experimental path. This was less the result of theory than an intuitional transmission, what D. H. Lawrence would have termed "blood-consciousness."

Like Kerouac, Creeley was a jazz enthusiast. He has stated that he spent much of the four years following the Second World War "frankly doing almost nothing else but sitting around listening to [jazz] records." He relished the memory of jamming with Kerouac at parties, drumming on pots and wine bottles on kitchen floors at three a.m., high in the belief that they were creating the most exquisite and ineffable sounds.

One of these parties reflects more innocent Beat pleasures. It occurred in April 1956. The occasion was a celebration of Gary Snyder's departure for a Zen monastery near Kyoto, where he would spend the next seven years as a lay acolyte. The guests sat in the horse pasture outside Gary Snyder's small burlap-lined cabin in Corte Madera in Marin County. This was where Snyder wrote "After Work" and "Marin-An" and many of the other poems that would appear in *The Back Country*.

Some of the partygoers smoked marijuana and listened to Cal Tjader records. Ginsberg played a recording of Henry Miller, one of the literary antecedents of the Beat Generation, who was cosmically rapping in a Brooklyn accent Ginsberg found endearing. Later, Kerouac and Creeley began drumming on pots while Ginsberg and Peter Orlovsky danced naked—"flowers at the prom" in Creeley's humorous image.

Michael McClure, Boulder, 1982.

Poet, playwright, painter, Michael McClure is an exemplar of Ezra Pound's famous injunction for artists to "Make It New!" In October 1955, McClure was one of the poets who read at the Six Gallery, an auto repair shop converted into an art gallery with black walls, a dirt floor, a makeshift plywood dais, and some surrealist sculpture made of orange crates and plaster-dipped muslin. This reading launched the San Francisco Renaissance and more than any other single event announced the arrival of the Beat Generation.

Using his art shamanistically to explore what he has called an alchemical consciousness, McClure is an avant-garde figure best known for his play *The Beard,* a magnetic dialogue between Billy the Kid and Jean Harlow, archetypes of violence and sexuality engaged in a mythic circular dance that seems particularly American. The play ends in a scene of graphic cunnilingus, and the right to perform it was challenged. In *The Beard,* in his peyote vision poems, and in an extended sexual poem called "Dark Brown," McClure has helped redefine what is permissible in American art.

Consorting with musicians and painters as well as poets and members of the Hell's Angels motorcycle club, McClure was a friend of Doors singer Jim Morrison. He told me that because of his fascination with Artaud, and in his own drive to venture beyond the frontiers of what was considered acceptable as drama, he brought Morrison to watch The Living Theatre perform *Paradise Now* in Los Angeles and San Francisco in 1969. The sensational nudity in the play and the audience participation onstage provoked Morrison into the mock exposure in Florida that so abruptly ended his performing career in America.

Some of McClure's incantatory poems have entered a mysteriously experimental nonmimetic space in which words are felt as pure sound rather than existing exclusively as units of meaning, as in Gertrude Stein or the end of Kerouac's *Big Sur* when Dulouz, Kerouac's fictional persona, tries to imitate the sound of the sea.

When I interviewed McClure for John Antonelli's film on Kerouac in Boulder in 1982, I asked him about Kerouac's extraordinary handsomeness in the period before *On the Road* was published. McClure, who is also remarkably good-looking, told me he identified with Kerouac because of his appearance. As a high school student in Kansas, McClure remembered, he would walk across the cafeteria with his neck so tense he could hear it creak because of his self-consciousness. He thought Kerouac must have been equally sensitive and aware of himself.

Edie Parker met Jack Kerouac in 1944, and she was so immediately infatuated she devoured six sauerkraut hot dogs. It was an act Kerouac admired because of its complete lack of self-consciousness.

Edie was raised in Grosse Point, Michigan, a wealthy suburb north of Detroit, and her father was a tycoon who owned hotels, shipyards, and textile mills. Feisty, fun-loving, in search of excitement—Kerouac called her "aggressively alive" in a letter—Edie came to New York and met Joan Vollmer Adams. Soon these two young women were living communally with Kerouac, Burroughs, and Ginsberg in a six-room apartment near Columbia University.

Edie Parker and Jack Kerouac had a mercurial relationship that included other lovers. When Kerouac went to sea, Edie got pregnant. Uncertain who the father was, she had an abortion.

Kerouac was later arrested as a material witness after the fact of a murder committed by Lucien Carr, one of his friends. Carr had stabbed a man named David Kammarer, who had relentlessly pursued Carr all through the summer of 1944 in an unrequited homosexual passion and who tried to assault him one night in Riverside Park. It was the first "ring of iron," Ginsberg observed, around their circle.

Outraged at this betrayal of family honor, Kerouac's father refused to help post a bail bond. Although Edie lived on a trust fund, she did not have the available cash for Kerouac's bail. Her father's lawyer agreed to provide such funds only after a marriage, which occurred on August 22, 1944, at City Hall. Kerouac's best man was a detective he had charmed while he was held pending bail.

The newlyweds took the train to Grosse Point; the train was so crowded Kerouac sat on the flag-draped coffin of a dead serviceman. It made him aware of how many of his young friends from Lowell had been lost. At Grosse Point, they were met by a chauffeured Packard limousine. Kerouac, whose mother worked in shoe factories, felt awkward in the presence of mansions, servants, and the plush Parker surroundings. Edie told me he spent the mornings sequestered in a bathroom reading Shakespeare and writing.

The marriage did not last long, but Edie, like many of the women involved with Kerouac, never seemed to have fallen out of love with him. In Boulder, Edie told me that Kerouac telephoned regularly until his death. If a man answered, he would rage, "Get out of my wife's bed, you bastard!"

Kerouac is prominent in the photograph taken in Edie's room in Boulder. When I asked her what personal details remained in her memory, what she remembered were his sad blue eyes that often seemed on the verge of tears and, incongruously, his favorite snack of cold asparagus, mayonnaise, and ripe olives.

Original manuscript of ON THE ROAD.

The torrential power of *On the Road* was a function of how it was finally written. Kerouac was inspired by a twenty-thousand-word digressive, unpunctuated, unrevised letter written in three days by a stoned Neal Cassady.

Kerouac was living with his second wife, Joan Haverty, in a loft owned by his friend Bill Cannastra, who had died in a spectacular subway accident when he tried to exit from a moving train and was crushed against a platform column. John Clellon Holmes described the floor-through loft in his novel *Go* as having "low windows, several grimy skylights that opened out on chimneys, and a sort of kitchen alcove in the back. It was always a fantastic litter of broken records, dusty bottles, mattresses, a slashed car seat, a few decrepit chairs from empty lots, and stray articles of ownerless clothing."

During a period of three weeks, in April 1951, Kerouac wrote at breakneck speed, typing relentlessly, so quickly he decided there was no time to change individual sheets of paper in his typewriter. So he fashioned a 120-yard home-made scroll by taping together twenty-foot strips of teletype paper he found in the loft.

He worked with very little time off for sleep, drinking cup after cup of coffee. To stay awake, he removed strips of Benzedrine from nasal inhalers that were then available in drugstores and dropped them in the coffee. The Benzedrine made him sweat profusely, and the loft was littered with discarded T-shirts. He was so concentrated in his purpose that, like Melville's Bartleby, he isolated his desk with a screen.

The manuscript was a single paragraph, using dashes instead of commas, the real names of his friends, and only a few periods. It was the first example of Kerouac's "spontanous bop prosody." When it was completed, he rolled it out on the floor, he wrote Neal Cassady, "and it looks like a road."

Carolyn Cassady has been both muse and maid of the Beat Generation. As a result of her marriage to Neal Cassady, she was a beleaguered woman, though there is a blitheness in her own account, *Off the Road,* that belies this impression. Despite her husband's reckless promiscuity, she stretches for respectability.

Daughter of a professor of biochemistry, a student of drama and costume design at Bennington College in Vermont, she had a middle-class background, and as Neal Cassady admitted in a letter to Jack Kerouac soon after he met her, she was a bit too straight for him.

Carolyn was in a graduate theater arts program at the University of Denver in the spring of 1947 when she was to some extent both deceived and charmed by her opposite, a man with "talking eyes." Neal, a natural grifter, was already married to sixteen-year-old Lu Anne Henderson.

Both Ginsberg and Kerouac were in Denver at that time: Ginsberg in amorous pursuit of Neal, and Kerouac in a more literary pursuit, since Neal had become the subject of his fiction. Appalled that summer when she discovered Neal in bed with Ginsberg and Lu Anne, Carolyn fled to San Francisco.

Cassady was one of the great talkers of his time, and he pursued her with letters that flowed like his speech. He persuaded her to marry him on April Fool's Day, 1948. With Neal working as a brakeman for the Southern Pacific Railroad, the couple had three children, including John Allen, a son named after both Kerouac and Ginsberg.

In 1951–52, while Kerouac was writing *Visions of Cody,* his second book about Neal, he moved in with the Cassady family in San Jose, California, and an undeclared, awkward *ménage à trois* ensued.

When *On the Road* appeared in 1957, the friendship between Neal Cassady and Jack Kerouac cooled considerably. Cassady may have felt that Kerouac had appropriated some of his spiritual energy. Another possibility is jealousy over Kerouac's tender closeness with Carolyn.

Neal Cassady was sent to San Quentin in 1958 for two years as prisoner # A 47667 for allegedly presenting two marijuana cigarettes to federal agents. Carolyn designed sets for local theaters and painted portraits, but needed welfare assistance.

She remained in contact with Kerouac until his death in 1969. In *Big Sur,* one of Kerouac's last novels, he speculates that Carolyn's karma was to serve Neal in this lifetime, although he quotes her as saying that she would get Kerouac in another life, and pursue him for eternities.

Carl Solomon and Gregory Corso, Boulder, 1982.

A "tough young kid from the Lower East Side who rose like an angel over the rooftops," as Jack Kerouac so aptly put it, Corso emerged from the street world of ordinary Beat misfortune to become an extraordinary poet.

Raised in orphanages and foster homes, he spent five months detained as a material witness in a larceny case and began sleeping on rooftops and in subways at the age of thirteen. By seventeen, he was in prison for theft, where he read Shelley.

Corso and Ginsberg met in 1950. Ginsberg approached him in a Greenwich Village lesbian bar, where Corso was sitting with a stack of the poems he had written in jail. The two young men discovered that they were unconsciously accomplices in a strange voyeurism: Corso had been masturbating while watching Ginsberg through the window making love with a woman named Dusty Moreland who lived across the street.

In 1954, Corso started auditing classes at Harvard and reading in Widener Library, an unofficial amateur student. He convinced a group of undergraduates to subscribe to the publication of his first book, *The Vestal Lady on Brattle.* This was an astonishing act of persuasion similar to that of Edgar Allan Poe, who, a century earlier, had convinced his fellow cadets at West Point to subscribe to his first book, *Tamerlane and Other Poems.* Autodidact, anti-mandarin, the bite-size absurdist poems of *Gasoline* were published by Ferlinghetti's City Lights, and then four books, including his best-known longer poems, "Bomb" and "Marriage," by James Laughlin's New Directions.

I had a revealing encounter with Corso after the party for Carl Solomon's *Emergency Messages,* which I edited in 1989. Like Solomon, who had once parked an ice cream truck in front of the United Nations and freely distributed its contents, Corso epitomized a surrealist buffoon role that could sometimes cross the lines of propriety or be recklessly hurtful. Corso was infamous for disrupting poetry readings as well as love affairs, and Kerouac dramatized both qualities when he portrayed him as Yuri in *The Subterraneans.*

The party for *Emergency Messages* was crowded into a small bookshop on Greenwich Avenue in the West Village. It was a warm fall night, and some of us had spilled out onto the street. Corso wanted to accompany me to a poetry reading in a garage on the Lower East Side. After about ten blocks, our cab paused for

a red light. Corso peered at me quizzically through his dangling grandma glasses, the wolf in Little Red Riding Hood trying to distinguish a shape in dense fog. In a grating voice he asked:

"Who *are* you, anyway?"

I admit I lost my sense of humor, a necessary quality for the appreciation of so puckish a gamin and *agent provocateur.* The moment seemed like a paradox in a strange dream. I felt like pumping him "full of lost watches," to borrow an image from his poem "Birthplace Revisited." I also felt angered enough by his tone of peremptory dismissal to exit immediately. I still wonder whether Corso had the money to pay the fare.

Lawrence Ferlinghetti, 1982.

Mellon read *A Coney Island of the Mind* when she was in junior high school, and she was one of thousands of young Americans it opened to the sense of liberation and joy that readers in France before the First World War experienced with Guillaume Apollinaire or readers of the Lost Generation with e. e. cummings.

Ferlinghetti's lyric, surreal, political poetry, along with his novels, plays, translations, and painting, has made him a unique international figure perpetuating freedom in all its manifestations. He represents as well a rare, engaged commitment evident in the bookstore and press he founded in San Francisco in the 1950s. City Lights became a model for the small press movement.

Ferlinghetti published *Howl* in 1956 and defended it in a famous censorship trial. His book and Ginsberg's have been the two most purchased and read books of poetry written by Americans in our time. So many have been moved by the resistance to the homogeneous and the eccentric stories of individual self-definition narrated in his poems.

Recently, walking my dog, Hunter, in the West Village, I met a former air force pilot, a big, tough guy I call Captain Bob, whose spirit had been sweetened by surviving a crash. It was a hot day and he was with his two Dobermans. I stopped to ask about the older dog, who was wearing incongruous homemade rubber booties on his paws to protect them from the pavement. Captain Bob asked me what I was planning for the summer, and I mentioned writing about the Beats.

Suddenly, in an operatic moment, he began quoting Ferlinghetti's "Dog," a poem about Ferlinghetti's own dog Homer, who once relieved himself on a policeman's leg and provoked the poem in which Homer is personified as the poet of the streets:

> although what he hears is very discouraging
> very depressing
> very absurd
> to a sad young dog like himself
> to a serious dog like himself . . .

I usually avoid Captain Bob, a weirdly wired guy with a deep year-round tan, but he kept me on the illogically intersecting corner of West Fourth and West Eleventh, quoting the poem and then explaining his passion for Ferlinghetti.

Anne Waldman with Diane di Prima, Boulder, 1982.

Diane di Prima offers the reminder that some liberated bohemians were women. As a nineteen-year-old poet, she initiated a correspondence with and then visited Ezra Pound, the poet who was incarcerated in St. Elizabeths in Washington, D.C., for political opinions he had voiced on Italian radio during the Second World War.

A second-generation Italian American, di Prima emphasizes the Beat preference for the knowledge of the street rather than the museum. An aspiring dancer, she told poet Anne Waldman that she grew up with a "tough back-to-the-wall, ready-to-fight-anybody attitude." Like Kerouac's, her first writing was in search of the vernacular, predicated on capturing the slang of New York in the early 1950s.

Di Prima helped edit *The Floating Bear* with Hettie and LeRoi Jones, a monthly newsletter, printed on a mimeograph machine in the back of a bookstore, that kept a vital poets' network alive in downtown Manhattan during the 1950s, a period of obscurity for them. Ginsberg, Corso, McClure, and Creeley all contributed. The mixture of gossip and serious aesthetic in *Floating Bear* was part of the definition of the underground and the beginning of the alternative press movement. When di Prima included a Burroughs routine in an issue, she was arrested by agents of the FBI on the charge of sending obscene material through the mail.

Hettie and LeRoi Jones, neighbors on the Lower East Side, published di Prima's first book, and she also had a daughter with Jones, another sign of a new lifestyle at the time. With the Poet's Press in the 1960s, di Prima published writers like Herbert Huncke and Timothy Leary. She also worked on key magazines like *Yugen* and *Kulchur* and in 1960 was a stage manager for The Living Theatre, the most politically outspoken drama group in the United States.

Diane di Prima is best known for her *Revolutionary Letters,* a book of poems about resisting oppression, published by Lawrence Ferlinghetti's City Lights Books in 1971. In *Memoirs of a Beatnik,* published two years earlier by Maurice Girodias's Olympia Press in Paris, she emphasized how small, ineffectual, and isolated her group was with its "unspoken sense that we were alone in a strange world." "High and delighted," she first read *Howl* on a pier on the Hudson River and then read it aloud that evening with a sense of discovery and exhilaration at a communal dinner. With a characteristic lack of self-consciousness, she remembers a subsequent night in a bed with Ginsberg, Orlovsky, Kerouac, and Corso, which she compared to the congeniality of sharing a warm bath with friends.

Ann and Sam Charters, Boulder, 1982.

Ann Charters is one of our leading Beat historians. Although she arrived as an undergraduate in Berkeley in 1953, she had not heard about the Six Gallery reading on Fillmore Street in San Francisco in 1955 where Ginsberg first read "Howl" while Jack Kerouac passed out gallon jugs of California burgundy, scat-singing and chanting "Go!" as encouragement.

Philip Lamantia, one of the other readers that night, observed that the effect of the poem was like joining two ends of an electric wire. "In all of our memories," Michael McClure remembered, "no one had been so outspoken in poetry before." Two days later, the reading of "Howl" was described in an article by Richard Eberhardt in the *New York Times,* which does not ordinarily concern itself with artists' gatherings on the opposite coast.

On some level, Ann Charters was surely listening. By 1956 she had moved out of a dormitory into a tiny, ramshackle wooden cottage, originally a gardener's shed, in the vicinity of Ginsberg and Gary Snyder. A friend arranged a blind date with Peter Orlovsky, who brought her to a repeat performance of the Six Gallery reading, this time in a Berkeley theater. She was enthusiatic about what she heard, though a bit unnerved by Robert LaVigne's drawings of Orlovsky and Ginsberg making love pinned on the walls of the theater.

As a graduate student at Columbia University in 1966, she visited Kerouac, who was living in Northport, Long Island, with his mother. When she began preparing a bibliography of his work, Kerouac told her, "I've kept the neatest records you ever saw." After his death, Rolling Stone Press published her biography of Kerouac. This was the first of almost a dozen biographies, and the most valuable because it established the historical record.

Recently she has added another dimension to her work on Kerouac by editing Kerouac's letters, *The Portable Jack Kerouac,* and *The Portable Beat Reader.* Eloquent and sincere, Charters teaches English at the University of Connecticut, Storrs. She met her husband, Sam, a blues historian, record producer, and novelist, in Berkeley in 1954 and raised two daughters with him.

Sam Charters told the following story about Mallay, one of his daughters, at the St. Mark's Church memorial for Ginsberg in 1997. In the 1960s, when Sam and Ann were living in Brooklyn Heights, Allen Ginsberg sometimes visited to talk about the blues. Ann and Sam always sang a little before putting Mallay to bed, and one night Ginsberg was so charmed by this he sang one of his renditions of

Blake for her in a very loud voice. Allen had a wild beard at the time, and Mallay went to bed a bit wide-eyed, but quickly and quietly.

Usually she woke her parents in the morning, but on the following morning she did not. Worried, Ann and Sam entered her room. Standing in her crib, gripping the rails tightly, Mallay demanded in a tense little voice:

"Is that man still here?"

When *On the Road* appeared in the fall of 1957, Kesey read it three times, impressed by its rhythmic power and the portrait of Neal Cassady. Three years later, when Kesey was a graduate student of creative writing at Stanford University, Malcolm Cowley was one of his teachers and an early reader of the manuscript of *One Flew Over the Cuckoo's Nest,* which Cowley recommended to Viking Press, just as he had recommended Kerouac's novel.

In 1962, six months after the publication of *Cuckoo's Nest*, Neal Cassady drove into Kesey's front yard in a battered Willys Jeep with a blown transmission, and became one of the core figures of the Merry Pranksters, the group of consciousness explorers formed by Kesey and described by Tom Wolfe in *The Electric Kool-Aid Acid Test.* Known as "Speed Limit" because of his unlimited use of amphetamines, Cassady drove the Pranksters from the West Coast to New York and back in a 1939 International Harvester bus painted in psychedelic Day-Glo.

Kesey's fascination with Cassady was as great as Kerouac's had been, and he wrote *The Day Superman Died* and the screenplay *Over the Border* in the attempt to understand him. After Cassady was found dead from an overdose of drugs and alcohol on the railroad tracks outside San Miguel de Allende in Mexico in 1968, Kesey concluded that Cassady's life "was the yoga of a man driven to the cliff-edge by the grassfire of an entire nation's burning material madness. Rather than be consumed by this burn, he jumped, choosing to sort things out in the fast-flying but smog-free moments of a life with no retreat. In this commitment he placed himself irrevocably beyond category."

Kesey was so drawn to Cassady because they shared an amazing charisma. I saw a flash of this magnetic energy when I invited him to read at Queens College in 1978. After I met Kesey at Kennedy Airport, we stopped at a diner for a bite. A stout man at the next table began wheezing and coughing, his face and neck turning red. The man slumped to the ground, and everyone in the place but Kesey froze. In an instant Kesey was on top of him with mouth-to-mouth resuscitation.

At the reading a few hours later, Kesey spoke in front of a room crowded with over a thousand students. One of them came up to the dais with his hand extended and, with a grandiose flourish, offered Kesey a joint. Again, there was a distinct freeze and a wave of apprehension. Calmly, deliberately, Kesey lit the joint and inhaled deeply.

Jack Micheline, Ken Kesey, and Ken Babbs, Boulder, 1982.

An Orphic figure, consumed by the power of his own song, Micheline was one of the great readers of poetry in our time. He took Jack London's first name as a means of identifying with the impoverished and outcast. Jack Micheline was a poet of urgency and exhortation in the vagabond troubador tradition of Vachel Lindsay and Maxwell Bodenheim. When he died in San Francisco in 1997, he was destitute and living in a flophouse.

In 1957, he was living in the same tenement in the East Village as Howard Hart, a poet and drummer who began the jazz-poetry scene with Kerouac and David Amram. Kerouac often crashed at Hart's flat, which was where Micheline showed Kerouac his first manuscript, *River of Red Wine.* Kerouac responded enthusiastically. In a generous introduction, he recognized an immediate affinity with what Kerouac termed his "swinging free style," praising Micheline's poems about bowery life, the illuminating beauty of the everyday, his soulful tender rage and enormous disappointment in the glut of a poisonous American materialism.

In the photograph, Micheline is relaxing on the porch of the Chautauqua Lodge. An old three-story bungalow with a hive of tiny rooms, situated in a complex of other old structures and a dining hall, the Chautauqua housed many of the Kerouac Conference speakers and performers. Robert Frank filmed *This Song for You, Jack* on the porch of the Chautauqua Lodge, asking the conference participants to remember Kerouac.

Much of the social life of the conference, rollicking and reminiscing over beers and smokes, occurred on this twenty-five-foot-square porch. Mellon and I had a room on the second floor, just to the side of the porch, and some nights we heard conversations that lasted till early morning.

Gregory Corso, Abbie Hoffman,
Johanna Lawrenson, unidentified student,
and Timothy Leary, Boulder, 1982.

Psychedelic pioneer and proselytizer, Timothy Leary gave Allan Ginsberg and Peter Orlovsky psilocybin, a drug derived from what are popularly called "magic mushrooms," when Leary ran the Center for the Study of Personality at Harvard in 1960. Ginsberg passed the drug on to Thelonius Monk, Dizzy Gillespie, poets Charles Olson and Robert Lowell, and Jack Kerouac, who tried it in Northport on the day of Kennedy's inauguration and described the experience as a magic-carpet satori. When Leary gave psilocybin to Corso and Burroughs in Tangier in 1961, Burroughs found that Leary was naive, that his hopes for a general instant enlightment were ridiculous, that what he called an "ersatz immortality" in *Nova Express* was at best a hoax and at worst a potential government tool for mass control.

Drugs as well as the Beats triggered the sixties counterculture, and Burroughs and Jean Genet did visit the Chicago Democratic Convention in 1968 as Tiresian witnesses. Ginsberg exerted a calming, nonviolent, chanting presence during the ensuing riots. Abbie Hoffman, one of the organizers of the protests at the convention, was tried with the Chicago Seven as a result, and like Leary later went through a period as an underground fugitive.

The most overtly political of the Beats during the 1960s, Ginsberg later admitted that the counterculture only aggravated American neuroses, that because its gestures emanated more from anxious outrage than love, it confused the political situation.

Fernanda Pivano with Joyce Johnson in background, Boulder, 1982

Fernanda Pivano represented a crucial European link to the Lost Generation because as a very young and beautiful woman, she had been an intimate friend of Hemingway's. A novelist herself, she is one of Italy's leading literary journalists, and has written a column in the *Corriere della Sera* in Milan for many years.

Nanda's specialty is American literature, and she introduced the Beats to Italy, hosting them and finding them publishers. She translated Ginsberg into Italian, and she organized a meeting over lunch between Ginsberg, Ezra Pound, and Pound's companion Olga Rudge, which led to the subsequent visit when Pound apologized for the "stupid, suburban prejudice of anti-Semitism."

She received *Naked Angels* very generously and went out of her way to describe each of my subsequent books in her columns. In the 1980s, Nanda would visit New York annually, and Mellon and I would often accompany her to dinner. Once Ginsberg joined us, even though he had just returned from Paris that morning and was unwell and exhausted. What Nanda wanted to know on her trips were the names of the new American writers.

In the fall of 1996, I was invited to be on a panel on the Beats at the Venice Film Festival. Nanda sat next to me, and spoke eloquently about how innovative the Beats had been, how their example had helped Europeans evolve from a stuffy formality in their writing.

We shared several meals at the grand Hôtel des Bains, which had been the setting for Thomas Mann's book *Death in Venice*. She was tormented because Ginsberg was encouraging a new Italian translation of his poetry that she interpreted as a repudiation of her own. She suspected a Machiavellian corruption in Ginsberg's ambition for a new edition. Her pain was considerable and harrowing. It strangely accented the haunting, plangent beauty of a Venice architecturally still frozen in the Italian Renaissance where I had lived in 1985, writing *The Solitary Volcano,* my biography of Pound.

I saw Nanda a few months later, and she was still agitated over what she regarded as a betrayal. This time she was in New York, because Ettore Sottsas, her former husband, was receiving a major design prize. She pleaded with me to intervene with Ginsberg, though I knew there was nothing that I could do. Life, for a writer, means remaining in print, and all translation is approximate and temporal.

Hello,
Mr. Nice Guy

Nothing is true, everything is permitted.

—Hassan-I-Sabbah

I   *The Majoon Prophet*

William Burroughs was unimpressed by fame and did his best to avoid its consequences. He had written, in *Naked Lunch*, a landmark of postmodernism that had begun as letters to his friend Allen Ginsberg. Writing in Tangiers under the influence of heavy opiates and majoon, a hashish confection, he described the fantasies, debilitations, and terrors of addiction from the inside. This was an audacious subject matter in the 1950s, but even more important was his startling departure in form. He had written an antinovel juxtaposing a series of mordantly bizarre burlesque sketches—he called them "routines"—all fragmented, discontinuous, expressing a hallucinated conspiratorial vision with surreal hyperbole.

Burroughs predicted our catastrophic national appetite for drugs. In 1947, he attempted to grow opium on a ninety-acre spread he had purchased in East Texas, a bayou area with pine woods, low rolling hills, and weather-beaten farmhouses. Opium does not grow north of the Rio Grande, but secreted between rows of alfalfa, Burroughs grew a crop of poor-quality marijuana. With Neal Cassady at the wheel of an old jeep, Burroughs drove to Times Square and sold it, anticipating a contraband business worth fortunes today in states like Georgia, Arkansas, and Hawaii.

In a series of fictions drawn from life though disguised through a prism of paranoia, he revealed our unlimited capacity for violence and the repercussive dangers of police surveillance and state control. He was, in short, an American Orwell, though like Tiresias, whom the gods installed in a bordello with the attributes of both sexes, he had to suffer to attain his vision.

II   The Ugly Spirit

I met Burroughs in the spring of 1974. The writer, known as "El Hombre Invisible," had recently returned to this country after more than two decades of self-imposed exile in Tangier and Europe. He was living in what he called the "Bunker," a cavernous, windowless, former YMCA locker room on the Manhattan Bowery, the street of derelicts and dead dreams.

I had published an essay full of praise for *Naked Lunch*. Although by reputation Burroughs was supposed to be glacial, I wanted to interview him for the book I was writing on the Beats, and I was nervous about it. I surmised, from reading a letter written to Allen Ginsberg in 1952, that Burroughs could be hostile: "I never swallowed the other cheek routine, and I hate the stupid bastards who won't mind their own business. I like very few people, as a matter of fact, and what happens to people I don't like, like the song says, ' 'tis their misfortune and none of my own.' "

Burroughs sat at the end of a long table. He was diffident, punctiliously self-contained, and cool as a knife blade. He stared right past me into a middle distance, and he had little patience for small talk.

I felt a crusty brittleness. It might have been a residual class affectation that reminded me of T. S. Eliot, and he told me he had seen Eliot read while he was in residence at Harvard when Burroughs was an undergraduate there. Burroughs was wearing mortuary colors: a black shirt, no tie, a three-button wool vest, and matching black trousers. It resembled the banker's look I remembered from photographs of Eliot, but it seemed curiously out of place, a disguise of sorts. My unease was furthered by a dry irritated edge to his tone; he kept punctuating my queries with an impatient "Next!"

To my consternation, Burroughs insisted that because of stylistic differences he should not be identified with the Beat movement. American writers despise classification and category. I realize that Hemingway or Fitzgerald would have offered similar disclaimers had they been associated with the Lost Generation. Burroughs was an iconoclast, an extreme individualist who lacked the qualities of sympathy so prevalent in almost all the other Beats, but the evidence of his participation in Beat history was overwhelming.

As a group, writers tend to be competitive and independent. I have already mentioned that in 1944, as a sign of the unusually close kinship of the Beats, Burroughs shared a large communal apartment with Kerouac, Ginsberg, and several women. Burroughs would use Kerouac as a sort of conduit to Ginsberg, who later became his agent and, for a brief space, his lover. In 1944, Burroughs collaborated with Kerouac on an unpublished novel called *And the Hippoes Were Boiled in Their Tanks*. Impressed by his ability as a raconteur, Kerouac predicted that Burroughs would one day write a novel called *Naked Lunch*, and over a decade later, in Tangier, he would help type it.

I knew that Burroughs was colder, more cunning and calculating, than Kerouac. After all, he had once declared that love was a "fraud perpetrated by the female sex," a notion Kerouac, by inclination always more of a romantic, would never accept. Burroughs was the factualist who represented an uncompromising truth, even to the point of hurtfulness.

When he met Kerouac in 1944 he surmised—quite correctly, as it turned out—that Kerouac was so emotionally bound to his mother he would never be able to leave her either physically or spiritually. In a letter to Ginsberg written in July 1958, he suggested, with one of his brilliant medical images, that Kerouac had been "sewed up like an incision" by his mother, a woman Burroughs categorically dismissed as "a stupid, small-minded vindictive peasant."

A man seemingly devoid of sentiment, Burroughs was much less interested in the past than in the present, and I recalled that in the "Atrophied Preface" at the end of his masterpiece, *Naked Lunch*, he had suggested that he was trying to write without memory. An intention of such immediacy is rare among writers. Burroughs acknowledged that he did not share Kerouac's interest in spontaneity, although in an undergraduate course at Harvard he had been fascinated by Coleridge's use of opium as a means of facilitating a writer's flow.

Mustering all my courage, I asked him to describe the circumstances of his fatal shooting of his common-law wife, Joan Vollmer Adams, in Mexico City in 1951. I knew this disastrous event was a personal fulcrum for Burroughs, the wound that finally precipitated his art. He had been a blocked writer for years, but at the age of thirty-seven, during his trial, he wrote his first books, *Junky* and *Queer*, a book published much later. Burroughs winced, then mumbled a reply while moving out of range of my tape recorder. I practically had to read his lips. It was an enormously uncomfortable moment for both of us.

When *Naked Angels* was published in 1976, Burroughs complained about my portrait of him, which he felt exaggerated his family's money and connections. He claimed I had been seduced by Kerouac's mythmaking, although I knew about a letter he had sent Kerouac from Tangier in September 1954 that mentioned the "St. Louis Country Club set" in which he had been raised. Ginsberg had confirmed this perspective in interviews with me, and it is clear that both Ginsberg and particularly Kerouac, with his lower-working-class background, saw Burroughs as affluent.

In *Naked Angels,* I wrote that I thought Burroughs had the "hauteur of an aristocrat who has known the gutter," which was the impression he gave me when we met. I had never mentioned the fact that his parents were listed in the St. Louis Social Register, and that his mother's brother, Ivy Lee, who owned a townhouse just off Fifth Avenue and who had been John D. Rockefeller's publicist, was listed in the New York Social Register. His daughter Alice, Burroughs's first cousin, had been presented in London at the Court of St. James's. If that wasn't a social connection, what was?

Burroughs's grandfather was a Princeton graduate who had perfected the adding machine by incorporating an oil cylinder. He dissipated much of the money he received from the Burroughs Corporation before dying young from tuberculosis and alcoholism. But Burroughs and his older brother attended private schools, his family moved to a big house situated on a five-acre lot when he was ten, his parents had a summer house and employed a maid, a butler, a nanny, a cook, and a gardener. When Burroughs was fifteen, in 1929, his parents took their two sons to France for a grand tour in a chauffeured car. His father had the good sense to sell a quarter of a million dollars' worth of Burroughs stock just before the Depression (the equivalent of several million now), so both boys could attend Harvard during its depths and receive an allowance long beyond graduation.

Of course, no one in the Burroughs clan ever was as wealthy as the Rockefellers. Like F. Scott Fitzgerald, Burroughs was *haute bourgeoisie,* on the fringes of the very rich, attending the same schools but invited only to the larger parties, while at the same time snubbed for never having quite enough money. His best friend and neighbor in St. Louis, Kells Elvins, was the son of a former congressman who was born in a town in Missouri named after his family, but Burroughs's mother ran a shop. Although he was raised in privileged circumstances, his exclusion from the inner circles of the very wealthy—which he regarded as a sort of primal disinheritance—gave him a crucial ambivalence about class and money.

What is interesting about Burroughs's reaction to the biographical portrait I offered in *Naked Angels* was his overreaction, and the myth of himself on which he insisted. It reminded me of Henry Miller's belligerent assertion that the protagonist he had imagined in his novels was literally autobiographical. In fact, as his friend Michael Frankel observed, Miller habitually distorted everything. Miller, for example, would tell the story of how his first mother-in-law had seduced him while she was bathing, a perfect fantasy of violated taboos for his fiction, but hardly what happened.

Burroughs chose for himself as his writer's capital the mantle of the heretical outsider formerly assumed by Ezra Pound—the invective in "Canto XIV," Pound's famous attack on British culture, should be seen as one source for Burroughs's rage.

On some level, Burroughs refashioned elements of his background to fit the myth that served him so well. Very early in life, Burroughs developed an intense self-loathing, which may be traced to his Welsh nanny. Like Miss Jessel in Henry James's *The Turn of the Screw,* she probably initiated him into sexual improprieties that no child should witness. His sense of himself as peculiar may have been intensified by another family servant, an old Irish cook who believed in the occult, concocted witchlike spells, and taught him the repulsive sorcery of emitting a high-pitched sound that could attract toads.

Like Kerouac and Ginsberg, and, for that matter, both Pound and Henry Miller, Burroughs had a major problem accepting his mother. It drove him to a psychiatrist after he was quickly discharged from the army during the Second World War. Throughout his life he experimented with various eccentric therapies, from Reich's orgone box to Scientology, probing the personal consequences of a dominating mother and a reticent, ineffectual father. Burroughs said that his mother had been "crippled by her Bible-belt upbringing" and decided that she projected a "tremulous look of doom and sadness," which is a poetic way of saying she was a terribly depressed person. Laura Lee Burroughs was frequently ill, and Burroughs claimed she was psychic, but she usually got her way. In her gift shop in St. Louis and later with an antique business in West Palm Beach, she served women who were much wealthier than she was. She also composed three books on floral design for Coca-Cola, in an ironic sense providing the writer-model her son would one day emulate.

Burroughs saw himself as a misfit, a detestable creep, an unwholesome child, "a walking corpse" as he described it in a repeated anecdote, so any hint of glamour or good fortune contradicted his self-made image as the marginal man, the Outsider, even the pariah like Tiresias. Alone among his peers as an undergraduate at Harvard, he kept a pistol in his drawer and a ferret as a pet, discouraging visitors.

When he shot Joan Vollmer in Mexico City at close range in 1951, he was suffering from what he described in *Queer* as a nightmarish depression. He claimed he was seized by a recurrent "ugly spirit" with which he would always struggle. In a letter to Ginsberg, dated March 18, 1949, a year before the shooting, Burroughs wrote that his relationship to Joan was from the beginning at an impasse and "not amenable to any solution."

In *On the Road*, Kerouac offers a tight glimpse of Burroughs *en famille* when Sal visits Joan Vollmer and Burroughs, Old Bull Lee in the novel, in New Orleans. The scene is based on a visit Kerouac made in 1949. Kerouac comments on the strangeness of the relationship with Joan, which Burroughs dominated with a dreary, monotonous monologue. Kerouac, always too generous depicting his pals, decided Joan's attachment to Burroughs was "delirious," resulting in an unfathomably "deep companionship," and what seemed "curiously unsympathetic and cold between them was really a form of humor."

In the scene, Kerouac also catches Burroughs's fixation with guns as he shows Sal his arsenal and boasts about a German gun that fired a gas shell capable of killing a hundred men. A practicing marksman, Burroughs always used weapons. He confessed to Ginsberg that the "William Tell act"—asking Joan to balance a glass on her head in Mexico City in the fall of 1951 so that he could shoot it off—had been his idea. When the Mexican police arrived, his unbelievable story was that the loaded gun had fallen off the refrigerator when its door had been slammed during an all-night party.

In a letter written several years after the shooting, sent from Tangier in February of 1955, he speculated that it was as if Joan's "brain *drew* the bullet toward it." Later, in what I regarded as a romantic rationalization, Ginsberg supported this view, telling me he thought Joan was "asking to be suicided" out of a relationship that was no longer tenable.

I have never forgotten a glimpse of the "ugly spirit" I discovered in the Ginsberg Deposit at Columbia University when I was doing the research for *Naked Angels*. A self-portrait by Burroughs done in charcoal with two large black circles for eyes, with calligraphic marks emanating from a black hole of a mouth, it looked as if Kafka's Joseph K had drawn it in an anguish of uncertainty, or in a fit of pain. Spectral, haunting, the drawing was a Rorschach test containing all the expressionist horror of Kokoschka, the ominous eeriness of Francis Bacon, the silently savage no-exit warning to stay away of Munch's *The Scream*. This was a man like Conrad's Kurtz, who had seen "the horror, the horror," and didn't particularly want to gossip about it.

III   The Burroughs Cult

I saw Burroughs on a few other occasions in the early 1970s, at a reading at the West End bar near Columbia University, where the Beat writers used to drink, and in 1973 while auditing a creative writing class he was teaching in place of Kurt Vonnegut at City College.

Burroughs felt that creativity could never be taught. Writing was learned by writing, provided the writer had certain requisite talents. For him, creative writing courses were just a faddish university scam. They were primarily useful as employment for writers who might otherwise be waiting tables, driving taxis, or fabricating jingles in advertising agencies if they were sufficiently gifted, as Burroughs had done for a time years earlier.

In class he was quite formal, always reserved, and only occasionally sardonic as he entertained himself with some observation that was often lost on his students. I heard no whisper of any of the maniacal characters he had invented. Instead he seemed like a decorous grandfather, though one burdened by some worry or terrible strain. The gentility seemed part of another disguise, a self-effacement that permitted him the novelist's role as observer. His students were disappointed, he surmised in an interview, because he wore a coat and tie to class, as if they "had expected me to appear stark naked with a strap-on, I presume."

The question he addressed was whether there was a "technology" for writing, as there was for physics, or engineering. Dogmatically, he preferred the word "technology" to "technique," its more humanist cousin. In his world, I sensed, it was better to use his vocabulary.

Once, when a student asked him about the postmodernist sacrifice of clarity and the consequent dangers of incoherence, Burroughs's reply seemed drawn from what he had stated in *The Job*, a collection of interviews about the craft of writing. Things didn't happen in a logical sequence in life, and "any writer who hopes to approximate what actually occurs in the mind and body of his characters cannot confine himself to such an arbitrary structure as 'logical' sequence."

He dominated the classes I audited with an old-fashioned lecture method, reading from carefully prepared notes that were more expositional than pragmatically connected to text. For a man who professed to despise intellectuals, he seemed very involved in theoretical possibilities for fiction—e.g., the cinematic way to present a story as opposed to one that depended on old-fashioned omniscience.

Hearing from Allen Ginsberg that Burroughs needed money, I invited him to read at Queens College. At dinner, he drank vodka and Coke, looked down at his food glumly, and barely spoke a word. Before the reading, in a stairwell, he insisted on lighting a joint, which he shared with two pale, thin young men whom he had brought along as sort of a straggling entourage. I must admit that that action made me, as an untenured member of the faculty, extremely nervous.

The reading was held on the top floor of the Student Union, which could accommodate around eight hundred students. Even with little publicity, the room was filled twenty minutes before the reading. When I scanned the crowd, I noticed a brooding element of pre-punk minimalism in the audience, sallow types and older black leather bikers who had heard through some esoteric grapevine that Burroughs was making a rare appearance.

I had asked him to read "Roosevelt After the Inauguration," one of his more outrageous Rabelesian parodies in which presidential cabinet offices are awarded to pimps, hookers, and thieves, and in which Burroughs imagines acts of copulation between a purple-assed baboon and some of Roosevelt's Supreme Court justices. Burroughs's delivery was crisp and his timing was electrifying, but I was apprehensive about how the bitter parody of his message would be received. At that time, the borough of Queens was still quite conservative. Through the 1960s, the effort in Vietnam had been patriotically supported in Queens, and Burroughs's more jaundiced views surely were suspect in such a place.

I saw him read again in the fall of 1978 at the Nova Convention. Organized on the Lower East Side, the three-day festival featured punk-rock musicians, Keith Richards (who failed to show), performance artist Laurie

Anderson, and Patti Smith in a fur coat and iguana boots (but her bronchitis prevented her from singing).

Paul Bowles once remarked that the Burroughs legend existed in spite of Burroughs and not because he sought to pursue it. The most obscure member of the Beat group had suddenly been launched as a cult figure. In the 1970s he appeared as a cool cipher in the crowd on the cover of the Beatles' *Sgt. Pepper's Lonely Hearts Club Band* and was photographed by Andy Warhol, Richard Avedon, Robert Mapplethorpe, and the conceptual artist Les Levine. These manifestations of the Burroughs legend continued through the 1980s when he posed for a series of ads for Nike and the Gap, and played a priest in a role that seemed written just for him in Gus Van Sant's film *Drugstore Cowboy*.

At the Nova Convention the word was that Burroughs—one of the few to break the most powerful habits of all—was back on heroin. He looked confused, gaunt, and frail. In the spotlight, his skin had a ghostly translucence. It was the first appearance of the "scarecrow suspended from a coat hanger" that James Wolcott would later commemorate in *The New Yorker*.

Led by acolytes to the front of a rowdy standing-room-only crowd, Burroughs was being figuratively crowned by countercultural worshipers, many of whom were unable to concentrate long enough to read his complicated prose. They seemed to revel with him as an icon in the way they might have with a David Bowie or a Lou Reed—two singers who were clearly influenced by him. I wondered whether I was the sole member of that audience who was disturbed by the fact that Burroughs slurred frequently as he read.

IV   All Supermarkets Look Alike

I did not see Burroughs again until the Kerouac Conference celebrating the twenty-fifth anniversary of the publication of *On the Road* in Boulder in 1982. Conducting a series of interviews for a film on Kerouac, I met him at the opening of an art show featuring Kerouac's paintings. When I asked him about them, he compared their rough uninformed power to van Gogh.

The room was full of undergraduates in short skirts swirling around with trays of hors d'oeuvres and martinis. Burroughs was quite drunk. Weaving and balanced by a cane that seemed in his hands like a formidable weapon, he was full of a manic, almost diabolic glee that I would see again when he performed one of his characters, Dr. Benway, with a grinning skeletal malice for Howard Brookner's documentary film on Burroughs.

That performance was a moment that seems more threatening in the post-AIDS era. In *Naked Lunch*, Benway is presented as an expert in mind control. As a surgeon, he represents authority, and in Burroughs's world such figures usually abuse their authority or sell it to the highest bidder. In a scene of hilariously grotesque pandemonium, Brookner showed Benway botching an open-heart surgery by using a toilet plunger to massage the heart. As a result, copious amounts of blood splattered all over Benway's smock, the anesthesiologist, and the nurse (played by Candy Darling, a transvestite who had been featured in some of Andy Warhol's films). All the way through, like some skinny version of W. C. Fields, Burroughs performed with a deadpan, snarling rancor, his voice an arrogant sneer full of caustic impatience and rage.

Burroughs told me something else at the Boulder art opening that I found startling. He had moved from the Bunker to Lawrence, Kansas, because of his friendship with James Grauerholtz, a tall, handsome young man who was his secretary and companion. I asked him whether the move from the East Coast to the plains in the middle of the country had any effect on his imagination. His answer had the impact of a blunt weapon hitting a soft object. With a devastating flatness that discouraged any further inquiries on my part, he replied, "To us lone cats, all supermarkets look alike."

I believe in distinctions and articulating differences when they exist, and at first I found his answer more puzzling than accurate. In Boulder, I had seen for the first time an enormous liquor supermarket bathed in what seemed like a million watts of fluorescence. So all supermarkets did not seem alike. Later, I realized that Burroughs's remark came from a man who inhabited an interior space that ultimately was all that he found interesting.

Burroughs was reluctant to be interviewed for my film, but when Ginsberg agreed, and after a lot of negotiation with Grauerholtz, he consented. On camera, he was terse and perturbed. I knew there had been an undeclared rivalry with Kerouac, who represented the heart and who had once accused Burroughs of being all mind. Burroughs kept looking sideways and twitching, body language that told me he could not wait for the interview to terminate.

V A Stick of Dynamite

One of the aborted interviews I attempted for the Kerouac film in Boulder was with a minor Beat poet named Ray Bremser. I remember a photograph of Bremser by Burt Glinn, part of a piece Kerouac published in a slick magazine called *Holiday*, in October 1959. Bremser is standing in the middle of the Gaslight, a coffeehouse on MacDougal Street in the honky-tonk part of the Village, reading poems to an intent audience. Even though a couple of his auditors are wearing sunglasses, Bremser seems uncertain and curiously out of place.

A rangy, hawkish man, Bremser had been incarcerated for armed robbery at the age of eighteen and had written much of his first book, *Poems of Madness*, in a cell. Bremser wrote a second book of poems, *Angel*, on light brown toilet paper in another jail cell. In Veracruz, Mexico, fleeing a court appearance, he encouraged his wife, Bonnie, to support him and their infant daughter with prostitution, a story she tells with graphic pain in her memoir, *For Love of Ray*.

Bremser had been a drinking buddy of Kerouac's, and like Neal Cassady and Gregory Corso, he epitomized the fast-talking, rollicking, street-hipster, con-man reckless abandon Kerouac romanticized with his glorious roman-candle image for madness early in *On the Road.* Ginsberg, taking this even one romantic step further, saw madness in *Howl* as insurgence of natural ecstasy rather than as the pain suffered by his mother, Naomi.

Bremser was especially edgy and surly, full of a coiling tension I found weird. He didn't quite know why he was talking to me and sized me up as if I were an FBI informant. It was a suspicion I recognized from trying to interview people like Lucien Carr and Herbert Huncke. When Bremser sat down, I noticed a bulge in his glossy high leather boot and asked him about it. Turning almost cheerful, he pulled out a stick of dynamite and explained that western miners provisioned themselves in this manner because they used explosives in their work, and for potential claim jumpers.

Bremser's aura of unpredictable irresponsibility scared me, so I abruptly discontinued the interview. The story is relevant in terms of Burroughs, who represents the dangerous, the less than beatific, side of the Beats. Poets like Ginsberg, Gary Snyder, Philip Whelan, Anne Waldman, Diane di Prima, and Kerouac were serious about Buddhism, but their ability to relate to more incendiary figures like Bremser and Neal Cassady is a sign of the mutual tolerance that helped the Beats cohere.

I suspect Burroughs was the sort of man who might have shouted fire in a crowded theater. What he distrusted most of all was what he would have called the lie of liberalism, which from his libertarian perspective only led to the poison of bureaucracy. "I tell you," he advised Kerouac in a letter from Mexico City dated on the Ides of March in 1949, "we are bogged down in this octopus of bureaucratic socialism." Bureaucrats, he told Kerouac in another letter written a few weeks later, are "a cancer on the political body of this country which no longer belongs to its citizens."

Such sentiments form the thematic argument of *Naked Lunch.* The strongest indictment of what Burroughs saw as the Trojan horse of liberalism occurs in yet another letter to Kerouac written on the first day of 1950:

> Allen [Ginsberg] is aligning himself with a cancerous element
> that will stifle every vestige of free life in the U.S. You notice
> that any oppressive, meddling piece of legislation (anti-gun,

anti-sex, anti-kick laws) is always loudly supported by the "Liberal" press. The word Liberal has come to stand for the most damnable tyranny, a sniveling, mealy-mouthed tyranny of bureaucrats, social workers, psychiatrists and union officials.

Burroughs once told me that the problem with liberals was that they thought they could legislate evil out of the human character. His fear was based on what he saw as an encroaching police state, although it chillingly anticipates the recent armed resistance of figures like Timothy McVeigh and far-right, so-called freemen Ayran supremacist groups in the western United States and racist, xenophobic skinheads and hooligans in Europe and America.

Burroughs, and Kerouac too, with the extreme and often inconsiderate individualism of the characters in *On the Road* and the alcohol-inspired political views he blurted in his final years, represent a curious conservatism that seems to cut against the grain of the Beat myth, at least as it is popularly conceived. Burroughs particularly is deeply suspicious of a Big Brother state apparatus that invents rules to govern all activities. This is what the Puritans did when they first settled the northeastern part of America, regulating everything from speech to dress and mandating attendance in church, but they were not able to put a video camera in every room!

VI   Hassan-I-Sabbah

Burroughs is the most extremist of the Beats, because his vision offers no hope. Americans, he believed in his singular fashion, were karmically afflicted and cursed because they had dropped the atomic bomb on Hiroshima.

Burroughs has been our most apocalyptic American writer since Edgar Allan Poe. Marshall McLuhan, reviewing *Naked Lunch* in *The Nation*, observed that criticizing Burroughs was very much like finding fault with the demeanor or dress of the man who was banging on your kitchen door to warn you that your house was on fire. It still seems an apt simile.

Burroughs is our plague artist. The French actor and writer Antonin Artaud proposed that the origin of Greek theater was not in the orgy, as Nietzsche had speculated in *The Birth of Tragedy*, but in a plague that leveled all social distinctions and created a need for rituals of purgation.

Burroughs has a less redemptive view of the unifying possibilities suggested by the plague than Artaud, Kafka, or Camus. The plague state leads to a delirium that is Burroughs's ideal moment, the point at which anything indeed is permitted and nothing seems true, when all distinctions and moral considerations are pointless. Much of Burroughs's fiction anticipates our fears of biological and viral warfare in the twenty-first century, as well as the emphasis on the social controls by the state that are the consequence of such fears.

The plague state is so harrowing because it offers us a historical analogy to the place we imagine as hell. Burroughs consistently explored its recesses from *Naked Lunch* on, and one of his last novels, *Cities of the Red Night*, is full of the exotically turbulent purgatory that for so long has characterized his world.

The opening scenes, depicting a death village permeated by a radioactive virus and a hospital epidemic of sexual delirium, present typical instances of Burroughs's vision, a perspective that sees entropic disease as the correlative to disorder and breakdown around us. Burroughs brings back for brief appearances certain favorite figures from his former fiction: Dr. Benway, still devoted to germ warfare; Lupita, the junky whore queen of *Naked Lunch*; Captain O'Brien and the Katzenjammer Kids.

Burroughs's characters move in a swirling ambiance of masturbation and ejaculation, of nooses, hangings, and gallows fornication, of astrally projected intercourse and sexual mutilation, of headless men fed through the rectum and used as love slaves, of sex nettles and orchids growing in human flesh, of pouches made of human testicles, of snakes, scorpions, centipedes, and the depraved smiles of idiotic lust appearing everywhere.

Surely the printing press of the future will produce Burroughs's novels complete with the smells and stains of semen galore: "A Firsty Pop is the hyacinth smell of young hard-ons, a whiff of school toilets, locker rooms, and jockstraps, rectal mucus and summer feet, chigger lotion and carbolic soap—whiffs you back to your first jackoff and leaves you sitting there on the toilet—"

Burroughs always gave us sights, sounds, and smells with an insistent clarity, sometimes unsettling his readers with a lurid lyricism. His voice is often laconic and his sentences spare so that the images flash forward all the more brilliantly. These qualities are evident in *Cities of the Red Night* as well as the attempt to relate a story in the juxtaposed fashion of Faulkner's *The Wild Palms,* in which two narratives are played off against each other.

In *Cities of the Red Night,* the first story is set in the eighteenth century as a band of pirates follow some libertarian calling and try to free South America from Spanish oppression. The story is intriguing, involving opium culture and transvestite crews (who entice merchant ships and then overpower them) under the leadership of the effeminate but ruthless Captain Strobe, who develops his revolutionary program in a Conradian setting. Burroughs's theatricality has never been so pronounced (with giant battles and orgies) as Strobe's crew, as various in national origin and ingenuity as Captain Ahab's, rallies to the buccaneer revolution.

Counterpointed to this story is a seamy detective melodrama. Private investigator Clem Snide pursues the trail of a hippie coke dealer who has been decapitated in a brutal sex crime. As readers of Burroughs's fiction know, his characters metamorphose and several voices can exist as aspects of an evolving identity, and so it is no wonder that Burroughs finds ways to join his pirate adventure to Snide's investigations.

Just when Burroughs has us tantalized, halfway through the novel, and without ever resolving either narrative, he introduces the Cities of the Red Night, a group of six fabulous places existing in the Gobi Desert one hundred thousand years ago that destroy one another and the planet in a cataclysmic war. Strobe, Snide, and the other time travelers of Burroughs's fiction participate in this frenzy that involves a CIA plot to exterminate humanity and rebuild it with a white gene pool.

Plot, in Burroughs's hands, is evidently in the service of an imagination that works mythically rather than historically, and his novel is full of parallels to Circe and Pan, to tarot figures, to arcane Egyptian and Mayan magic rituals. In Burroughs's hand such staples of fiction as plot and character are invariably reinterpreted so that critics complain that his characters resemble cartoons more than they do rounded, realizable, even identifiable humans. Such criticism seems quite beside the point, for Burroughs is a postmodernist fabulist, not an imitator of Dickens. And postmodernism, as even so suspicious a historian as Gertrude Himmelfarb has observed (*American Scholar*, Spring 1997), proposes a radical relativism, a skepticism so absolute as to reject such notions as greatness or even the idea of truth.

For the postmodernist, she alleges, "there is no truth, no knowledge, no objectivity, no reason, and, ultimately, no reality. Nothing is fixed, nothing is permanent, nothing is transcendent. . . . What appears to be real is illusory, deceptive, problematic, indeterminate. What appears to be true is nothing more than what the power structure, the 'hegemonic' authority in society, deems to be true."

Himmelfarb could almost be describing the epistemology governing *Cities of the Red Night*, or the motto of one of its characters, Hassan-I-Sabbah, that because nothing is true, anything is permissible —the nihilistic refrain that appears often as a personal maxim in Burroughs's letters.

An eleventh-century Persian religious agitator who founded the Ismaili sect, Hassan-I-Sabbah was known as "the Old Man of the Mountain" because he lived in a fortress located at an altitude of ten thousand feet near Teheran. As an archetypical terrorist, he trained teams of young assassins who used hashish ritually, and who, in turn, were controlled by Hassan-I-Sabbah through its use. Hassan-I-Sabbah first appears in *Naked Lunch* and reappears as one of Burroughs's prototype code figures, an anarchist from the larger social perspective who used focused control systems to achieve his ends.

Control, irrespective of any relative morality, is the game of the power state. Of course, the "morality" of any time or place is itself the ideological underpinning of any system, the basis for any set of social controls. Manipulation and control were Burroughs's perennial concerns from the time of his studying the Mayan codices in Mexico City in the early 1950s, and Hassan-I-Sabbah and his hashish assassins provide another locus point for Burroughs's fascination with how events can be shaped.

Burroughs interprets Hassan-I-Sabbah's principle as a license for free-dom. To the extent that modern life depends on manufactured illusion—achieved through media manipulation and state management—any illusion is feasible and permissible. To arbitrarily and exclusively establish any single view as "real" is to exclude any other possibility.

Burroughs's view is that "morality" never depends on any innate prin-ciple, and the law of any state merely exists as a function of its power. To paraphrase Oscar Wilde, morality is something we usually apply to those whom we personally dislike.

Hassan-I-Sabbah's motto, however, seems valid only from the Dadaist perspective. Nothing indeed may be "true" in any enduring sense, neither the crumbling pyramids nor the words on this page, which are subject to interpretation. However, using that indeterminacy to justify the conclu-sion that everything is permitted sounds like one of those desperate blind leaps in the dark that Henry Miller was always exhorting his readers to take. Most of us are far too cautious for that sort of plunge, either blindly or with open eyes. When a writer like Burroughs invites us to enter his sable world, we may do that more with our eyes open than with our hearts receiving.

VII   A Quicksilver Daredevil

Norman Mailer, a writer not given to praising his contemporaries, once remarked that Burroughs was the only writer of our time to have been possessed by genius. "Genius" is a word that writers use too frequently, but the key word here is "possession," and some part of Burroughs's drug use, certainly his use of the hallucinogen *ayahuasca* that he found in Peruvian and Colombian backwater towns in 1952, has to do with the telepathic states he believed drugs could induce and his interest in magic. Herbert Huncke, who initiated Burroughs into the world of drugs in 1944, told me that Burroughs was interested in hypnotism when he met him, another more personal control system bordering on the magical that could be used to affect events.

The essayist Seymour Krim once characterized Burroughs as a "quicksilver daredevil," and I think that phrase captures much of the trickster craft in Burroughs's imagination. The evolution, for example, of Burroughs's technique from the journalistic naturalism of his first novel, *Junky*, to the pyrotechnical virtuosity of *Naked Lunch* is remarkable.

Like Joseph Conrad's, Burroughs's major problem as a writer was an emotional blockage, which he overcame only with the shooting of Joan Vollmer. Murder, whether accidental homicide or assassination, is surely a drastic remedy for what is the most common disability faced by writers. The point is that Burroughs would continue to have difficulty releasing his story. He did not have the extraordinary fluency of a Kerouac, who could compose an entire novel like *The Subterraneans* in an athletic seventy-two-hour period and never write two novels in the same style. Burroughs was the sort of writer who had to pay for every word.

Some of this payment was epistolary. As Oliver Harris so astutely suggests in his introduction to *The Letters of William S. Burroughs*, much of *Naked Lunch* is anticipated or proposed in the correspondence with Ginsberg. Juxtaposing the letters with fragmentary material and other "routines," he realized his mosaic architecture. But the letters reveal an ongoing struggle. "It is extremely painful," he wrote to Ginsberg on October 10, 1955, "trying to weld all this scattered material into some sort of coherent pattern," and he repeats the word "pain" three times in this letter alone.

The use of the "cut-up" followed *Naked Lunch*, which may have creatively exhausted him. Burroughs announced the cut-up technique as a means of new linguistic discovery, a castration of the continuum of meaning that might allow a text some autonomy of its own, some escape from the manipulative control of the writer. The term "cut-up" specifically applies to the scissors Burroughs would use to splice into his text the passages from Rimbaud, Conrad, or T. S. Eliot, passages he would select and arbitrarily integrate into his narrative without explanation or acknowledgment. The term suggests as well the anarchistic humor of a man acting on a stage, a burlesque of form for the sake of exposing pretensions. By inserting into his text passages by other writers, Burroughs joined the tradition of accidental art that began with Duchamp and was continued by the Dadaists and then by John Cage and Jackson Pollock.

In one sense the cut-up eliminates a potential for pretentiousness or self-consciousness. It is consistent with what Burroughs told Ginsberg on first meeting him in 1944. Ginsberg, still very much the Columbia undergraduate, asked for a definition of "art." Burroughs's reply was tersely factualist— "Art is a three-letter word!"

In another sense the cut-up is his mechanical rejoinder to the warmth of Kerouac's spontaneity. Philosophically, it is his attempt to violate what he called the word lines of Western conditioning and the linearity of old-fashioned art in the way any fundamentally new artistic form affects perception. Psychologically, it was an expression of his increasing detachment from human involvement as well as a way to overcome the paralysis of being unable to continue writing.

The unreadability of the cut-up device dominated and nearly destroyed the value of *The Soft Machine, The Ticket That Exploded,* and *Nova Express,* the three novels that fulfilled the *Naked Lunch* tetralogy. To his credit, Burroughs realized the dangers of sacrificing any potential audience, and in his novels of the sixties, particularly in the compelling *The Wild Boys,* he returned to more narrative priorities. But even in *Cities of the Red Night* and the novels that followed, he continued to use the cut-up selectively.

Burroughs was introduced to the cut-up by his friend Brion Gysin. The two men became friends in Paris in 1958, when Burroughs was assembling the material that would be published as *Naked Lunch.* Burroughs told Allen Ginsberg that Gysin's paintings were "the psychic landscape of my own work." The cut-up method, Gysin stressed, treated words in the way a painter treated paint, as raw material with its own rules.

Gysin's impact on Burroughs was profound, and the calligraphic drawings Burroughs did in Paris in 1958 for the dust jacket of the first Olympia Press edition of *Naked Lunch* reflect the Arabic script and the Japanese calligraphy that Gysin studied. With Gysin in the 1960s, Burroughs worked on photomontage scrapbooks. For several decades, Burroughs collaborated with Gysin and a series of other painters, often contributing texts. Robert Sobieszek, who was curator of the show of Burroughs's paintings for the Los Angeles County Museum of Arts in 1996, has aptly characterized Burroughs's own paintings, mostly conceived in the 1980s, as works of "expressive automatism" resulting in surrealist *terrains vagues* or mindscapes.

In the early 1980s, Burroughs began blasting a double-barreled Rossi shotgun at a can of paint placed in front of a canvas or plywood panels. I saw some of this work at the Tony Shafrazi Gallery in Soho and found it both compelling and disturbing. At first I found it difficult to connect Burroughs's painting experiments with his writing, and I wondered whether the visual had replaced the verbal as a source of inspiration.

Chance, which has been more important to painters than writers, was the connecting link. Burroughs once told me that the final order of the routines that formed *Naked Lunch* was accidental. Maurice Girodias, publisher of Olympia Press in Paris, gave an editor named Sinclair Beiles two weeks to help Burroughs assemble his chaotic manuscript. Burroughs would read a routine, and if they liked it, it was placed on a table. At the end of two weeks they had selected enough material for a book. When Burroughs asked about the sequence of the routines, Beiles said there was no time left, and he left them in the order in which they were stacked. The progression from chance order as an artistic principle to the random effects produced by a shotgun blast on a panel of paint seems like a natural evolution.

In an essay entitled "Painting & Guns," printed as a miniature book by Hanuman Books in 1994, Burroughs explains the relationship of the visual to the verbal in his work:

> Because it is read sequentially, there is no way to effectively portray simultaneous events in writing. But that's the whole point of painting: multiple points of view can be simultaneously presented. One expands the area of awareness, and one seeks new

frontiers in randomness. A shot gun blast produces explosions of color that approach this basic randomness.

Burroughs used a surface of slick paper that enabled the colors to run, and instead of brushes he used his fingers, mushrooms, Pollock's drip device, and a series of other randomizing techniques to increase the accidental or chance aspect of whatever would ensue. His argument, a recapitulation of Cézanne's study of changing light, is that while the artist statically tries to remember a scene or to paint it, everything is changing. So the result is only an abstraction. Burroughs's interest was montage, which was much closer to the facts of perception for Burroughs than any representational art because it locates the reader in the flux of change as it occurs, and as such comes closer to suggesting an illusion of actual process.

VIII   Dream Magic

Burroughs, whose maternal grandfather was a preacher, reminded Jack Kerouac of a "Kansas minister with exotic phenomenal fire." Appropriately enough, perhaps, he spent the last fifteen years of his life in the quiet college town of Lawrence, Kansas, a place once pillaged and burned by the notorious James Gang.

Burroughs died at the age of eighty-three on August 2, 1997. Surprisingly, for a man who had consumed as much alcohol and drugs as he had, he lasted considerably longer than the biblical allotment of threescore and ten years. Laid out in an open cherry-wood coffin in Liberty Hall in Lawrence, he wore a tawny-colored velvet Moroccan vest Brion Gysin had given him, and on its lapels were pinned his honorific florets from French and American academies. Someone read Alfred Lord Tennyson's "Ulysses," one of Burroughs's favorite poems. A professor from the University of Kansas department of religion spoke about freedom. There was music: Schubert's "Fantasie," Moroccan joujouka, "St. Louis Blues" sung by Bessie Smith. Just before the casket was closed, a pistol and a joint were placed inside. The next day, the body was driven in a white hearse to the Belle Florette Cemetery in St. Louis, where it was buried in the Burroughs family plot, near the monument to his grandfather established by colleagues of the Burroughs Corporation.

Burroughs remains our ultimate sorcerer of fiction, a space-age Poe inhabiting a landscape of nightmare. Critics already have begun to speculate that the dense thicket of his writing will make Burroughs unreadable in the future, or at best to be skimmed or sampled. Such a facile argument has been leveled at all the modernists, from Pound to Joyce to Faulkner. Hallucination should hardly make easy reading, and Burroughs's audience has always been more select than Kerouac's.

The most surprising thing that I heard when I met Burroughs in 1974 was his insistence on viewing art as a magical form. He argued that in the world of magic, nothing happened unless someone willed it to happen, and there were certain magical formulae to channel and direct the will. What we call "art," he explained in his bone-dry gravelly monotone, was magical in its origins, employed for ritual or ceremonial ends to produce definite effects.

Naked Lunch originally was to be about what Burroughs characterized to Ginsberg as an "anti-dream drug," a force used for the sake of control that would destroy the "symbolizing, mythmaking, intuitive, empathizing, telepathic faculty in man." Without the freedom to dream, to conceptualize the new, we become somnambulists in space, no more adept than soulless robots. For Burroughs, the dream faculty lies at the very heart of what artists want. In *Painting & Guns* he points out their purpose is to "dream for other people," presumably even for those who can no longer dream for themselves.

What I admire in Burroughs's work is a spirit of stubborn insubordination that refuses to accept the machine or its robotic agents no matter how efficient they may seem. If Burroughs's obsessively parodic focus on the manipulative games of what he calls the Control Forces frightens us at all, the warning is beneficial, even when it seems bestial.

Pierre Rouyer and Brion Gysin in Paris, 1985.

Experimental writer and self-taught painter, Gysin was Burroughs's collaborator and close friend. Gysin knew he was an artist as a young man, and in Paris in 1935, at the precocious age of nineteen, he exhibited his drawings with a group of the surrealists until expelled from the gallery by André Breton.

In the U.S. Army during the war, he studied Japanese, which became a formative influence on his brushwork. He wrote a history of slavery in Canada and then traveled to Europe on a Fulbright Fellowship. On the advice of Paul Bowles, in 1950 he moved to Tangier, where he opened a restaurant called the 1001 Nights, observed Moroccan sorcery, and overlaid Arabic script with Japanese calligraphy in his paintings to form a cabalistic grid that resembled language.

Although he met Burroughs in an art gallery in Tangier in 1953, the friendship developed in Paris five years later when he accidentally encountered Burroughs on the street. Burroughs was trying to make his *Naked Lunch* manuscript cohere, and was living in a small forty-room hotel at 9 rue Gît-le-Coeur near Notre-Dame. Gysin rented a room, and discovered the cut-up while slicing through a pile of newspaper and randomly piecing together the fragments.

In an interview in *Rolling Stone* in 1972, Gysin argued that all Western religions depend on language and sequential order, which the cut-up could radically alter. With Burroughs he produced *The Third Mind* and *Minutes to Go,* books of theoretical and practical extensions of the method.

Despite his misanthropic reputation, I found Gysin both congenial and engaging when I visited him in 1982 on the rue Saint-Martin, just across from the Pompidou Center in Paris. Gysin had been made a Chevalier of the Order of the Arts by the French government, but he was completely unassuming and unpretentious.

In 1987, a year after Gysin's death, his second novel, *The Last Museum,* was published by Grove Press. Grove had been bought by Ann Getty, the oil heiress, whose son Peter admired Gysin.

I was asked to review the novel for the *New York Times Book Review*. Perhaps excessively influenced by Joyce and Burroughs, it presents a complex series of grotesque dreams, mostly rendered in dialogue, involving graphic sexual fantasies with figures like Gertrude Stein and William Burroughs in a Paris hotel like the one at 9 rue Gît-le-Coeur.

After I submitted my review, Nona Balakian, an editor on the *Book Review,* complained to me that the *Times* was a "family newspaper" and that they could not print my piece. I wanted Gysin to receive the notice that had been denied during his lifetime, so I had to avoid mention of the more bizarre sexual rituals that Balakian found distasteful.

It did seem like an object lesson: almost thirty years after *Naked Lunch,* what happened in the dark recesses of Gysin's fiction could still not be illuminated in the mainstream press.

Norman Mailer, South Londonderry, Vermont, 1970.

Novelist Norman Mailer has a very tangential relationship to the Beats. He shares their fear of the dangers of totalitarian tendencies and technology. He did speak brilliantly for the defense of *Naked Lunch* in court in Boston in 1965, and his novel *Why Are We in Vietnam* (1967) shows Burroughs's influence.

His celebrated essay "The White Negro" originally appeared in *Dissent* in the summer of 1957, just before *On the Road*, and it was then brought out as a slim book by Ferlinghetti's City Lights. In his focus on the hipster as a potential source of revolutionary change in consciousness, the "sophistication of the wise primitive," as Mailer puts it, he was allied with Beat interests.

Mellon had been working as a stylist for Tosh Matsumoto, a still-life photographer who observed that she had a good eye and should take photographs herself. This photograph was her first self-assignment. We were staying at a friend's glass-walled chalet on Stratton Mountain in Vermont. Mellon heard that Mailer was renting a farm in the vicinity and boxing under the tutelage of José Torres, the former world middleweight champion. When she knocked on his door, it was opened by Mailer's mother, who warmly invited her in for some Russian poppyseed cookies.

Mailer was forty-seven years old and still in his Hemingway mode. He would do roadwork in the morning and then spar three rounds. On the morning this photograph was taken, he was beset by a muscular, aggressive twenty-five-year-old bartender, a Golden Gloves contender, who wanted the reputation of having knocked the famous writer on his back.

Mailer feinted, grunted a lot, backpedaled for three rounds, but succeeded in staying on his feet. I helped remove his gloves, and I noticed the thumb on his left hand was entirely dislocated. The pain was reflected on his face. When I asked Mailer why he had not quit, he replied that he "would never give that punk the satisfaction of saying I backed down."

Mellon and I spent a half-dozen evenings at the farmhouse. Mailer drank straight gin from a pewter tumbler, and we talked a lot about Henry Miller, another writer he admired. No matter how much he drank that summer, at least in our presence, he was perfectly mannered, candid, sweet-tempered, and considerate.

We met most of his visiting children from various marriages and his parents. I heard no raving, no boasting or malice, no overwrought obsessional rants, no instance of what has been called his enormous ambition. He could sound urgent or combative when defending Miller against the feminists, as in *The Prisoner of Sex,* which he had just written, but mostly he would listen with intense concentration, his mouth pursing as if he were trying to kiss your idea into existence.

Barney Rosset is one of the key impresarios of the Beat Generation. Son of a Chicago banker, Rosset was a photographer in China while serving in the U.S. Army Signal Corps during the Second World War. After the war, he produced a film about race relations, *Strange Victory.* In 1951, twenty-nine years old and attending the New School on the GI Bill, married to his prep school girlfriend, Abstract Expressionist painter Joan Mitchell, Rosset bought Grove Press, a tiny reprint house, for $3,000.

Inspired writers who had been rejected by every mainstream publishing house could find an audience through Rosset, who could sense the prophetic force of such figures. Interested primarily in the priorities of personal freedom, he published Brecht, Artaud, Jean Genet; he published Samuel Beckett's *Waiting for Godot,* the unexpurgated version of *Lady Chatterley's Lover,* and Henry Miller's *Tropic of Cancer.*

Miller was a personal mission for Rosset. He discovered a contraband copy of *Tropic of Cancer* in Frances Steloff's Gotham Book Mart, and wrote about it while feeling absolutely stultified as an undergraduate at Swarthmore. His professor pronounced him jaundiced and probably spoke for the country at the time.

The right to publish Miller was challenged in every state of the Union. Rosset fought all the lower court cases and five state supreme court cases. When the U.S. Supreme Court overturned all the lower-court rulings, Miller and Rosset had rewritten American publishing history.

Rosset has stated that publishers "are the foot soldiers in the struggle against hypocrisy and oppression." He believes that publishers should affect rather than simply reflect culture, and he subscribes to a broad-based avant-gardism. In 1957, he began *Evergreen Review,* featuring Ginsberg, Kerouac, and many other Beat writers. In 1962 he published the American version of *Naked Lunch,* which had originally been published by Maurice Girodias's Olympia Press in Paris. Again, his right to publish had to be defended in court.

At seventy-six, Rosset is a trim wire, lurching in electrical movement in the office of his new press, which is also his home. An old jukebox, hanging beads, and a pool table evoke an earlier, more hip era.

Still cool, he pours himself a triple scotch with Coke, moving incessantly, gesticulating as he talks about Paris, beginning with the story of a lunch where he introduced Miller to Beckett (who liked him), and then the memory of Allen Ginsberg meticulously correcting Maurice Girodias's impressions of Burroughs.

Rosset published several of Kerouac's novels, including *The Subterraneans*. When he first met him, Kerouac seemed like a street tough. He remembered another meeting, with the visiting French publisher Gallimard. Kerouac was chaste and sober, accompanied by his mother, whom he feared. She began playing the piano terribly and singing in what, according to Rosset, was her awful version of French. Gallimard was enthralled!

+   +   +   +   +   +   +   +   +   +   +   +

Look for the Diamonds in the Sidewalk!

. . . so **Kerouac** raved & prophecied & continued down his path thru the farm fields cursing the **Academics** who distorted his vision of **America** in the world—I trudged uphill marveling at his energy & enthusiasm and devotional madness . . .

—**Allen Ginsberg,** *Luminous Dreams*

I   A Generational Spokesman

Gilbert Millstein's review of *On the Road* in the *New York Times* early in September 1957 compared the novel to *The Sun Also Rises*, seeing both as signals of generational identification. The comparison would have been even more apt had Millstein compared Kerouac to F. Scott Fitzgerald rather than Hemingway, but Millstein's rave review placed Kerouac on the American literary landscape and made his novel a best-seller.

The review is an example of rare literary good fortune, and the power of the critic in formulating taste or discovering the new. Kerouac was lucky because Millstein, a music critic with an ear for jazz, was filling in for the paper's regular critics, who probably would have ambushed or dismissed the novel, had they bothered to review it at all. Certainly David Dempsey's piece a few weeks later in the Sunday *New York Times Book Review* was far more cautious and qualified than Millstein's.

The luck of the draw was that Millstein's review launched Kerouac, celebrated him, and earned him a notoriety that ultimately confused and plagued him. Although he had published his first novel, *The Town and the City*, an apprentice coming-of-age fiction set in his hometown of Lowell, Massachusetts, Kerouac had been an obscure unknown before Millstein's review.

A novelist is not identified as a generational spokesman unless able to dramatize the spiritual changes that define an era. *On the Road* was characteristically American in its search for a fluid, unshaped life, free of preimposed patterns, fearing most the horrors of convention, conformity and stasis, of staying in the same place without the courage to change.

In this regard what becomes central to any reconsideration of Kerouac is his view of his own country and the way his work was received by it.

II   Assimilations

One unifying theme for the Beat Generation is the Fall of America. Gregory Corso used the phrase in a poem called "Variations on a Generation," and I found it again at Columbia University in the early seventies, when doing the research for *Naked Angels,* in one of Allen Ginsberg's notebooks for 1957: "Therefore I prophesy the Fall of America / Bitter, Bitter tongue to tell."

During the Second World War, when Ginsberg, Burroughs, and Kerouac formed their first nexus, one of the books Burroughs encouraged his two new younger friends to read was Oswald Spengler's *The Decline of the West.* I suspect Kerouac may have been less taken than Ginsberg by the notion of the inevitable decline of any world power, the thesis that the moral cost of its expansion usually leads to a tragic enfeeblement.

Jack Kerouac was the son of working-class French Canadians, and his first language was joual, a French Canadian dialect. As the child of immigrants, Kerouac developed a particular kind of devotion to and admiration for America often found among immigrants and their children. This is a common ingredient in our national past, a motivating and energizing American quality, the fruit of immigrant cultures living in metropolitan ghettoes and assimilating a larger set of social customs. It can result in a kind of optimism that Whitman saw growing out of our melting-pot development through the nineteenth century.

I need not quote any sociological studies to support this; I can rely on a firsthand account. Born in Belgium on the eve of the Second World War, I was luckily brought here as a boy and became so fascinated with everything American I would spend a lifetime reading American literature.

As a child I insisted that I be called John, not Jean, my given name, and I studied every way—from pinball to baseball—to become an American as quickly and totally as I could. The first hurdle for me, as it was for Kerouac, who spoke English with a halting accent until he entered high school, was a matter of sound and linguistics. While at home I would hear my parents converse in French—which I had to understand if only to understand what they were saying about me. Their European accents, however, when they spoke English (which they both knew before emigration) were a secret source of shame for me. The sound of my American language as I voiced it had to convince my play companions or schoolmates that I was as native as they were. As kids in postwar New York City, we were particularly proud of being Americans.

I'm not suggesting that Jack Kerouac should be seen as a patriot: anyone who was scrutinized by naval psychiatrists in the mental brig has to have too complicated a story for so simple a formulation.

Although he was discharged after flinging down his rifle and walking off the drill field to read in the base library, he was still determined to serve his country during wartime. A half-dozen voyages as a merchant marine seaman, transporting the bombs and ammunition that sustained the war effort in waters patrolled by German submarines, helped him develop a mordant awareness of the brevity of life and its preciousness.

In 1945, when his father developed cancer of the spleen, Kerouac chose to care for him in Queens and missed a voyage for which he had signed on. The ship was exploded by a torpedo and all hands were lost. Had Kerouac been on board, it is possible that no one would have heard of the Beat Generation.

III   Listening

I find something quite revealing about Kerouac's attitude to America in an early letter written at sea to Norma Blickfelt, a Barnard College girlfriend. The letter is dated August 25, 1942, when Kerouac was working as a scullion. He had not seen Norma since April, and he nostalgically remembered a twelve-hour period they shared together, shortly before he left for a trip down south.

It is the brief description of this trip in the letter to Norma that interests me. Kerouac wrote that he "wandered about in my own lonely way, from city to city, village to village, listening to the Negroes sing the blues, eating and working in lunchcarts, hopping freights and listening to the great American music of a train whistle. I never did hit Asheville, N.C., Wolfe's hometown."

Several things seem characteristic: the lonely wanderer has Thomas Wolfe on his mind, but most important he *hears*, the real work of the novelist —the train whistle, the black blues, or the inflections of actual speech. This listening is related to an eye that could perceive a world of trolleycars and Cadillac fins Kerouac could still remember so nostalgically.

Henry Miller, who along with Hemingway was the American master of natural speech as opposed to the inflected, affected, artificial language some writers employ, noticed this facility of Kerouac's in his preface to *The Subterraneans*. Kerouac, he wrote, was "always alive to the idiomatic lingo of his time—the swing, the beat, the disjunctive metaphoric rhythm which comes so fast, so wild, so scrimmaged, so unbelievably albeit delectably mad, that when transmitted to paper no one recognizes it. None but the poets, that is."

This aural capacity reminds me of something a former minor-league ballplayer told me about Kerouac when I was interviewing people who had known him for John Antonelli's Kerouac film. The ballplayer met

Kerouac in 1965 in St. Petersburg, where Jack was living with his mother and his third wife in a two-bedroom cottage.

This ballplayer played right field. At that time the ballparks in St. Petersburg were still segregated, so if one was black the only place to sit was in the bleachers. Every day this right fielder was baffled by the presence of one white blip in the bleachers, and he finally talked to him, offering him a pass for seats behind the dugout. The white blip was Jack Kerouac, who dismissed the offer, saying that he wasn't as interested in the game as in listening to the talk of the black people around him. The ballplayer had no idea Kerouac was a writer, one who by then was past his prime, but who was working on *PIC*, a Huck Finn novel in dialect about a ten-year-old black kid, and depended on the conversational rhythms around him.

I think that kind of eagerness to hear, that receptivity to the music of language, has something to do with why the saxophonist Lester Young passed Kerouac his first joint in a taxi during the war. It is connected to a zeal, almost a Buddhist recognition, really, that never denies suffering but includes it as part of the music.

I guess this grounding in a universal sadness, as well as gospel roots, is why we often associate the word "soul" with jazz. Kerouac set a record cutting classes at Columbia because he would spend all night listening to Lester Young or Charlie Parker at Minton's Playhouse in Harlem, and then continued with after-hours sessions. Essentially, this young man from the province of Lowell, Massachusetts, was wordlessly learning the sounds of hip and making of it a new rhythmic basis for fiction.

The outsider in Kerouac allowed him to identify with those he called the "fellaheen," people of the third world and the dispossessed Native Americans—he claimed his great-grandmother was part Iroquois. It also helped him appreciate the struggle of the black community. That sort of identification was a function of openness as well as part of an inquiry—see Norman Mailer's essay "The White Negro"—into the sort of cultural differences that could inform any writer with an alternative value system.

John Clellon Holmes told me that the inexpressible exuberance suggested by jazz was "a call from the dark," a repository of black ways of coping with centuries of suppression in America, and at the same time a "euphoria of joy," released in the face of the blandness of Eisenhower's America.

In a piece called the "The Beginning of Bop," Kerouac remembered an evening at Minton's during the war listening to Thelonius Monk, Dizzy Gillespie, and Charlie Parker. The "chest shivering excitement" of the new sound they had discovered derived from swing, a prewar development in which the alienated black teenager became "the hep-cat, the jitterbug, and smoked the new law weed"—marijuana had been declared illegal only in 1937. Kerouac affirmed, and he was one of few white men to voice it so clearly, that bop was the language of America's "inevitable Africa," that is, a population that had been tacitly ignored and segregated for a century after the Civil War. Kerouac argued that the musicians knew that "Negroes in America are just like us," that even if they were still "misplaced and mis-noticed in the white nation," their aspirations were universally legitimate and human.

Kerouac's analogue for the writer became the bop saxophonist. Instead of playing a prescribed and set melody, the sax player would pursue a sound dictated in the moment, a variable and malleable sound, one that depended more on mood than mind, and that lasted as long as the wind of the performer. Kerouac applied such notions of breath to the extraordinary riffs he devised in *Visions of Cody*, his most adventurous fiction, though long considered his least publishable work.

An excellent illustration of the sort of rhythm he invented in *Visions of Cody*—progressing beyond syncopation to bop—is found in the proem to the "jazz-tea high" remembrance of Cody late in the novel:

> At the junction of the state line of Colorado, its arid western one, and the state line of poor Utah I saw in the clouds huge and massed above the fiery golden desert of eveningfall the great image of God with his forefinger pointed straight at me through haloes and rolls and gold folds that were like the existence of the gleaming spear in His right hand, and sayeth, Go thou across the ground; go moan for man; go moan, go groan, go groan alone go roll your bones, alone; go thou and be little beneath my sight; go thou, and be minute and as seed in the

pod, but the pod the pit, world a Pod, universe a Pit; go thou, go thou, die hence; and of Cody report you truly.

Kerouac's reliance on broad open vowels creates an incantatory sense of awe appropriate enough for any writer concerned with deity in an age marked by a cynicism so severe that practically no other American writers could admit such a concern. Kerouac's capacity to believe, however, should not be confused with innocence. In an astonishing remark, late in his life, Kerouac told an interviewer on national television that he was "waiting for God to show his face." His "wait" was with a certitude that represented one of the many polarities in his temperament and his fiction, and it represented a stabilizing balance for the sometimes frenetic searches of his overexcited characters.

IV   A Spontaneous Bop Prosody

One of the crucial keys to Kerouac is the question of spontaneity. By declaring that he would not revise anything he had written because God had dictated it to him—and how could any mere mortal change divine injunction?—Kerouac was baiting the entire literary establishment with one of its own shibboleths.

Revision is one of the sacred cows of the literary experience, and the craft it requires separates the professional writer from anyone with the human desire to tell a story. The furor over spontaneity begins with the inception of romanticism in England. William Blake, in his comment "of the Measure in which *Jerusalem* is written," began by remembering "when this Verse was first dictated to me"—suggesting problems that would only be compounded by the opium reverie in which Coleridge wrote "Kubla Khan."

The academic critics who do so much to fashion literary reputation in any age suspected an arrogance in Kerouac's "first thought, best thought" philosophy, and to some extent they were offended because the cautious calculation they felt was necessary for art seemed to have been willfully snubbed or sacrificed.

Kerouac could afford the risk of spontaneity because of the control he had developed as an apprentice writer with books like *The Sea Is My Brother*. As Burroughs observed, Kerouac had written almost a million words as a teenager, twice as many as are in *War and Peace,* so he had mastered much about the craft of writing. Consequently, as John Clellon Holmes maintained when I interviewed him in 1974, spontaneity was a way to free a writer from conventional approaches to fictional problems by relying on a totality of feeling and sensibility, emanating more from the heart than the mind, and incorporated in a flowing process that occurred best when the words and images cohered immediately, without reflection or searching.

The attitude that embraced spontaneity was the affirmative spark of the entire Beat movement, a surge of optimism in the face of the bleak fifties that was captured in the conversations of Kerouac's friends and characters. Holmes, in an article published as early as November 16, 1952, in the *New York Times Magazine,* characterized that particular energy as a "bottled eagerness for talk, for joy, for excitement, for sensation, for new truths." He recognized his nascent Beat friends by a "look of impatience and expectation" that signified "ungiven love, unreleased ecstasy and the presence of buried worlds within." The extreme energy of such eagerness was a counterpoint to the defeated, beaten-down qualities commonly accepted as the soul dimension of the Beat experience.

No wonder Kerouac could write *The Subterraneans* in three days and nights or *On the Road* in three weeks. The velocity of his compositional methods, the ability to commit to the sound of his mind as it streamed forward, without either hesitation or loss of confidence, contributed to what Helen Taylor—the Viking editor who reworked the long single-paragraph manuscript version of *On the Road*—called his lavish recklessness: "a torrential force that comes directly out of the material, instead of being applied to it, almost as if the author did not exist as an outside agency of creation."

Publication of selections of the more than 120 volumes of Kerouac's journals in *The New Yorker* and *The Atlantic Monthly* in 1998 illustrate the extent to which Kerouac had prewritten, as it were, sections of *On the Road*. Consider, for example, the famous "Lilac evening" section of the novel when Sal Paradise wanders through the black part of Denver longing to identify with the warmth and ease he feels in the neighborhood. This part of the novel was denounced by James Baldwin as patronizing, and applauded by Eldridge Cleaver as a sign of vital interest in how black people live. The heart of the section was written as a journal entry for August 1949. Large chunks of the rest of the novel were taken from journals written between the time Kerouac met Neal Cassady in 1947 and 1951, or passages Kerouac called "sketching" in which Kerouac transcribed events as they occurred.

Of course, there are fascinating changes, which the academic critics and their graduate students will begin to chart as soon as the Viking edition of the journals become available. The key line of the "Lilac evening" passage, for example, that the best that the "white world" had to offer did not provide sufficient ecstasy for Sal—"joy, kicks, music" are the terms he uses—were originally used to describe Kerouac's own disappointment after completing the editing of *The Town and the City,* a painful struggle for Kerouac because almost a third of the manuscript was sacrificed. In an entry in August 1949, he acknowledged that Robert Giroux, his editor, told him the "laurel wreath" was not a function of worldly acclaim but "worn only in the moment of writing."

That moment of writing was the spontaneous rush of pleasure Kerouac felt when one word propelled the next. Spontaneity was as important for Kerouac's own methodology as listening. I would compare Kerouac to the bop pianist Earl Bud Powell, who would stand on street corners with a notebook, transcribing the sounds of the street and mixing them with those in his head.

It is a misconception that jazz improvisers never repeat their solos. Actually, they often perfect solos on certain tunes, and then use them when they need them. When the writers Aram Saroyan and Ted Berrigan interviewed Kerouac for *The Paris Review* in 1968, they were surprised that he could, in a Zen instant, respond to their questions with a haiku. Of course, he had memorized his own haiku as well as Bashō's!

The truth is that Kerouac did revise, and there were several earlier attempts to write *On the Road*. The extent of his revision, of course, will become clear when all the manuscripts are annotated and published.

Spontaneity was a central Beat tenet, an expression of a radical honesty that suspected the element of artifice in literary process. Culturally, it was equivalent to Jackson Pollock pouring his paint directly from the can to the canvas, or John Cage accepting ambient sound in his compositions.

But it is important to realize that the spontaneity that Kerouac waved as his stylistic flag was just that, an ideal that was more spiritual and conceptual than an absolutist end. The goal of spontaneity was spiritual, Kerouac's response to the stuffy elitism in much fifties fiction, the studied elegance of psychological novels written by lifeless imitators of Henry James.

V   Whitman's Wild Children

Another musician, David Amram, told me that Kerouac used to remark as they walked down Bleecker Street in Greenwich Village, "Look for the diamonds in the sidewalk!" The sentiment may sound a bit incongruous, a slaphappy outrageous side of Kerouac, a counter to an equally present gloominess, deriving from the homespun zany surrealism of the Three Stooges, W. C. Fields, and the Marx Brothers, whom Kerouac loved on the screen when he was a kid in Lowell and to whom he traced some of the roots of the Beats in a talk at Hunter College on November 6, 1958.

But the remark is another key to Kerouac's perspective, which colored the way he saw America. It is an evocation of Whitman's notion that all life is holy miracle, and that what the artist has to do is listen, look, and wonder about it. Many of Kerouac's critics were initially put off by this glorification of the commonplace, not the more banal, neutral, and ultimately sensational use of the soup can in Warhol, but the sort of affirmation announced by Sal Paradise in *On the Road* about one of his companions who "began to learn 'Yes!' to everything, just like Dean at this time."

Whitman's view was panoramic, all-encompassing, always inclusive and expansive. As a journalist, he knew the seamier side of life, and he certainly condemned the unrelieved materialism of the period that followed the Civil War, but at the same time as a poet he exalted and embraced the vitality he sensed in a nation reaching for its powercrest.

With an affected, almost inebriated western swagger, Whitman referred to the island of Manhattan as "Manhattanoes," an endearing affectation that Kerouac adopted. There is a lot of Walt Whitman in Jack Kerouac, particularly a working-class outlook that Whitman derived from the Quaker farmers of his childhood and his work as printer, teacher, reporter, and carpenter. Kerouac's father also set type, and like Whitman, who started working as a messenger at eleven, Kerouac was a poor child.

In "Song of Myself," Whitman announced for America his own version of manifest destiny, a quest for national unity and individual transcendence that is what sets Sal Paradise off as a journeyman on his road. Whitman declared the road was a vehicle for traveling souls, and in making the road his primal metaphor, Kerouac exulted in a characteristically American mobility, an evocation of the freedom myth of the western frontier. No wonder the novel is replete with references to the mud or dust to which in the biblical sense we all return.

"Sal" is short for "Salvatore," a name associated with salvation. The deliberately religious imagery—how many times does the word "pilgrimage" appear?—Kerouac used in *On the Road* underlines the quest motif that organizes much of the picaresque action. In that novel the repeated vision of an inspired prophetic wanderer who moans for man, the long strophe sentences that determine its rhapsodic rhythm, the catalogs, the parallelism, the repetitions of words like "mad" and "sad" or the color red, or references to the stars, the deliberately ecstatic lyricism of scenes such as when he has a vision of his mother working in a Market Street diner in San Francisco, are all willful emanations of Whitman that point to a mysticism unfamiliar to our predominantly skeptical and secular literature. In the postwar period when the holocaust was seen as a confirmation of the absence of deity, the critics mistook the searching of Kerouac's characters for naiveté.

As a student of Buddhist belief—which the posthumously published *Some of the Dharma* so powerfully adumbrates—Kerouac accepted and in a manner courted death. One early personal myth of mutability, shared by Ginsberg, was a fantasy about an enveloping "Shrouded Stranger," which became an active principle in his novel *Dr. Sax*. The childhood death of his older brother, Gerard, the thrombophlebitis Kerouac developed as a young athlete, the bomb runs as a merchant seaman, and watching his father die of cancer all left him with a religious adoration for the sacred purpose of our abbreviated time on earth.

At the same time, like Whitman or our most romantic poets, he responded to the miraculous possibility of being alive, and was able to describe that passionately though always elegiacally. It is exactly that tension between celebration and elegy that is the most appealing aspect of Kerouac's strength as a writer.

VI   The Open Heart

John Clellon Holmes told me that Kerouac was the most openhearted writer of his generation. And it is a fusion of the awareness of suffering and the openness to miracle that I find the central binding force in Kerouac's attitude.

Kerouac grew up during the Great Depression, and in 1936 the Merrimack River, flowing through Lowell, overflowed its banks, flooding Leo Kerouac's small printshop. This was before federal protection programs for natural catastrophe. Leo was ruined, becoming an itinerant typesetter, ending up in Ozone Park in the borough of Queens, a working-class neighborhood of New York City.

Early in 1995, at the International Center of Photography in midtown Manhattan, I saw Dorothea Lange's photographs of unemployed men and impoverished women in Depression shacks, faces lined by life, toughened and marked with woe. Like Lange's, Kerouac's sympathies are with the working classes, even as many of his characters are dreaming of ways to avoid the work system to which most of them are bondaged. Unlike Steinbeck's agrarian migrants, who are desperate to work, Kerouac's wanderers are like Neal Cassady—consumed by the "disease of overlife," as Kerouac put it in his poem on Rimbaud. In both *On the Road* and in *Visions of Cody,* Kerouac mythologizes Cassady as the archtype of a reckless, freewheeling irresponsibility too Dionysian to be employable.

No wonder Kerouac so idealized the hoboes in *On the Road.* By dropping out of the materialist game, they have at least won a glimpse of freedom, even if it is illusory. This reminds me of another aspect of Kerouac's take on America—alone among American writers, except perhaps for Jack London, who was part of Coxey's Army of the unemployed in 1894 and published a book called simply *The Road* in 1904, Kerouac lived on the boweries of Manhattan, Denver, and San Francisco, existing on pennies a day and cheap wine. The beatness of that kind of experience has to be radically transformative.

When writers—think of Orwell or Henry Miller—survive the jeopardy of vagabondage, the vulnerability of compromised health, little or no money, and a sense of supplication only a mendicant can know, they can emerge with a more generous outlook as well as a story. To the extent that they are able to describe the suffering of a dispossessed underclass, they need to be able to transcend middle-class expectations of comfort, security, and status.

Consider, as a tiny example, a phrase from the second chorus of a poem called "San Francisco Blues":

Line faced mustached
Black men with turned back
Army weathered brownhats
Stomp on by with bags
Of burlap & rue
Talking to secret
Companions with long hair....

All through "San Francisco Blues," or "Mexico City Blues," which is more metaphysical, Kerouac offers a street perspective of vagrants and drifters, hustlers and whores, which differs from more naturalistic views of writers like Stephen Crane in his story "Maggie" or Dreiser because of its genuine empathy. Kerouac is not a tourist lounging on the street to seek a story, not a sensation-seeking journalist, but an intimate, as beaten down by the humiliation, chaos, and uncertainty of homelessness as any of his subjects.

VII   The Americans

In connection with what I have called Kerouac's working-class street perspective, I would like to consider a little piece in *The Portable Jack Kerouac* called "On the Road to Florida," an account of a car trip Kerouac took with the photographer Robert Frank in the late 1950s. This was the original introduction to Frank's classic book *The Americans,* which editors at Grove Press asked Kerouac to rewrite because it sounded too much like a short story.

Kerouac marvels at how Frank, whom he compliments as the Dos Passos of American photographers, shoots through his dirty windshield with one hand on the wheel, or suddenly stops to focus on a solitary light pole with a cluster of silver bulbs illuminating what he calls a "lorn American landscape":

> how beautiful to be able to detail a scene like that, on a grey day, and show even the mud, abandoned tin cans and old building blocks laid at the foot of it, and in the distance the road, the old going road with its trucks, cars, poles, roadside houses, trees, signs, crossings. . . . A truck pulls into the gravel flat, Robert plants himself in front of it and catches the driver in his windshield wild eyed and grinning mad like an Indian. He catches

that glint in his eye. . . . He takes a picture of a fantastic truck door announcing all the licenses from Arkansas to Washington, Florida to Illinois, with its confusion of double mirrors arranged so the driver can see to the rear around the body of the trailer . . . little details writers usually forget about.

Only Kerouac would have used that soulful "lorn," short for "forlorn," as in the "forlorn rags of growing old" at the very end of *On the Road* with its reiterated "O" forming a resonant biblical wail. But the piece is characteristically Kerouacian, the truck and its power driven by one of Whitman's "roughs" with a glint in his wild eye, a "real" American, heralded by an array of licenses that symbolize the rules that regulate us and the geographical contours of our Manifest Destiny. All this captured by Robert Frank in an uncontrived manner Kerouac could admire because it was so similar to his own technique of sketching events in the streets in a little notebook, and his own diarist's immediacy, his ability to write without filters or revision.

In his published Introduction to *The Americans*, Kerouac comments on Frank "with that little camera that he raises and snaps with one hand" so as to have "sucked such a poem right out of America." He defines what is so poetic about the moods in Frank's photographs in a ringing opening sentence: "That crazy feeling in America when the sun is hot on the streets and music comes out of the jukebox or from a nearby funeral. . . . " Frank had captured, as Kerouac put it so brilliantly, something as characteristically American and central to Kerouac's concerns as the "charging restless mute unvoiced road keening in a seizure of tarpaulin power." The sentence represents high tribute, particularly because Kerouac borrowed it from *On the Road*. Allen Ginsberg claimed it was the single sentence Burroughs most admired in Kerouac's work.

In "On the Road to Florida," Kerouac is constantly comparing the writer's opportunities to the photographer's and wishes for his own "mad, mental camera" to note the details that are the record of life in America. It is a lesson for any writer, Kerouac concludes, to follow a great photographer and look at what he shoots. The result is America, and "it awakens the eye every time."

The spontaneity of the photographs in *The Americans*, their uncrafted appearance, almost like glimpses from a passing car, had great appeal for Kerouac. Like Henry Miller in *The Air-Conditioned Nightmare*, a travel account based on revisiting America during the Second World War after a decade of expatriation, Frank probed the smiling surface of America to reveal an anguished solitude in the midst of community and a brooding alienation in the presence of plenitude.

Kerouac's kinship with Frank was based on a shared anti-elitist perspective that understood that the artistic source of power or beauty was as much in the streets as in the stars. Although in *The Americans* Frank resisted the romantic buoyancy of Kerouac's view, his subject was the same, an attempt to embrace the manifold heterogeneity of the American experience.

VIII   "The Joyous Disease"

In 1955, Kerouac wrote Allen Ginsberg that three of his favorite writers all ended as recluses, Blake, Thoreau, and Emily Dickenson. I think he was predicting his own future, but the perspective of the recluse, a bitter contradiction of the genuine warmth and compassion of his best fiction, certainly colors his views of America during his last years.

Kerouac's final take on his own country must be measured by the fact that he was first of all a poet who used the novel as his form. The terms of his last views are blurred by what he called "the joyous disease," the alcoholism that reamed him out at the end, which may have been the only solace for the loss of an enormous talent. Great American novelists do have peak periods: think of Melville in the early 1850s, Faulkner in the early 1930s, or Jack Kerouac in the early 1950s. Kerouac himself was fully aware of this, and in 1952 he exclaimed in a letter that "I have completely reached my peak maturity now and am blowing such mad poetry and literature that I'll look back years later with amazement and chagrin that I can't do it anymore."

What does the loss of such power imply for any artist who has glimpsed its intoxicating flights? Kerouac's emotional decline corresponds with his own awareness that he could no longer match his earlier inspirations. Like Henry Miller, Kerouac had a prodigious exuberance that often resulted in extremely prolific writing sessions that could produce up to five thousand words. In his early journals, like some Ben Franklin or Horatio Alger, he measured his daily output with a batting average. We often take the writer's effort for granted, and those of us who are not writers cannot know how depleting the work can be. Conrad or Hemingway, for example, would be mentally exhausted after five hundred words.

Henry Miller, who did his great work in Paris in the *Tropics* novels of the 1930s, had little inclination to continue writing when he returned to America after the war. He was more or less cajoled into *The Rosy Crucifixion*, a tepid retelling of the *Tropics* material, by Janine Lepska, his third wife, who thought her husband should be writing. Something of a similar nature occurred to Kerouac after the success of *On the Road* when his publishers asked for a sequel, which he gave them with *The Dharma Bums*. But *On the Road* had been written six years before its appearance in 1957, and Kerouac had already lost much of his power. On some level, he had to be aware of this diminution.

The best account of this mysterious change is provided by Kerouac's friend John Clellon Holmes. In 1951, when Kerouac finished the marathon three-week literary explosion that resulted in the scroll manuscript of *On the Road*, he brought it to Holmes to read. Holmes was so astounded by what he regarded as a major formal breakthrough that he spent the next year writing an imitation called *Go*. Kerouac's novel was rejected by several publishers, mostly because of his unorthodox manuscript and his refusal to consider revisions, and that stand practically cost him his entire literary career. Imagine how he felt when Holmes's forced, flat version of *On the Road* appeared in 1953.

It is a sign of Kerouac's extraordinary generosity that he forgave his friend and continued to see him until the end of his life. When interviewing Holmes in his home in Old Saybrook, Connecticut, in 1974, I read in his journals the most convincing account of Kerouac's notorious decline into a soured, mean-spirited, often delirious incoherence, a shriveling bitterness that precipated his early death at the age of forty-seven.

Kerouac stayed at Holmes's Old Saybrook house in the fall of 1962, while Kerouac was ostensibly house searching. Actually, during the last decade of his life —as a register of his personal confusion —he had relocated with his mother from Northport, Long Island, to Lowell, to California, and to St. Petersburg, Florida.

In the fourth day of the visit, Holmes noted that Kerouac was already up and drinking Courvoisier at nine. By afternoon Kerouac was napping,

that incredible, lava-hot flow of memories, imaginations, perceptions, nonsense and humor temporarily stilled. We ranted and argued . . . and I've been close to that unapproachable core again, and I actually think that he has had a good time. He is probably the most prodigious, indefatigable drinker I've ever known. His genius is exhausting, unique, volcanic, and is fed somehow by booze . . . his strange amalgam of spurious ideas, verbal illumination, cornball politics, dead certain aesthetic feeling, huge relish for life, fatalistic physical strength—all that I knew so well once, has come back to me in a rush. The horrors lie ahead for him tomorrow or Saturday, he knows it (having that queer strain of self-knowledge that is part of all real talents in our time). Our feelings towards one another remain ambiguous. We like one another enormously, we are so utterly different and disagree with great foaming screams. Anyway, I'm enjoying these wasteful, abusive days of literally hours and hours of frantic, drunken talk—one flowing into the other, all sequence and cohesion swept away sometime days and days ago. I try to keep shaved and reasonably sweet-smelling. Jack sits in torn blue pajama bottoms, a rank tee shirt, grimy socks and Japanese slippers, unshaven in nearly a week, his hair never combed until 5 p.m., growing headier and headier in the armpits, smoking his little Camels, fixing his brandies and soda, padding around with faltering old man's steps, talking in torrential gusts.

By this time Kerouac was drinking more than a quart of brandy and assorted chasers a day. The brandy stimulated him to the point where even barbituates like Nembutal did not slow him down. Kerouac had once boasted, in a journal entry written in August 1949, that he would "never give up, and that I'll die yelling and laughing" and this vociferous, rowdy energy was still present during Kerouac's last years.

He was still yelling on the visit to Holmes, but on some level he had surrendered, succumbed to what Joyce Johnson called "his vulnerability to profound loneliness and nearly suicidal despair" in her *Washington Post* review of the *Selected Letters: 1940–1956*. Way down deep, Holmes asserted in his journal account of Kerouac's visit, Kerouac wanted to die, "and no amount of self-abuse, disaster or sadness can expunge the feeling of loss and estrangement which has always scarred him." Such people, Holmes observed, leave a permanent mark.

For what seem totemistic reasons, we are fascinated by the alcoholism of modern writers, as if we were surprised that the personal or political disasters Hemingway, Faulkner, or Fitzgerald witnessed should have driven sensitive souls to temper their sorrows with alcohol. Joyce Johnson reminded me that Kerouac was a gifted mimic with a photographic memory, even to the point where he could reproduce entire conversations long after they had taken place. John Clellon Holmes told me in 1982 that anyone who could remember as much as Kerouac could—he called himself "Memory Babe"—would have to find a way to relieve himself of the burden.

But the "burden" was not merely a function of memory. While psychoanalytic terms offer at best only rough categories for human behavior, Kerouac had what some might today call a bipolar personality. This bipolarity formed the central tensions in his work as well as his outlook on his own life and the future of his country, just as it exists in the two great polar regions of our planet. In a journal entry written as a young man of twenty-five on New Year's Day, 1948, he observed that he had read the manuscript of his first novel, *The Town and the City,* and his opinion of it was similar to his view of himself: "gleeful and affectionate one day, black with disgust the next." The words suggest the optimism and brooding despair, the desperation to dance before the doom on the horizons that form the north and south poles of his fiction.

A little more than a decade later, in some kind of Dorian Gray reflex, Kerouac's deterioration became evident. Photographs taken in the 1960s document the way Kerouac's Montgomery Clift movie-star look of bruised vulnerability and dark intensity had become bloated into a Balzacian balloon, a distended, unbroken belly beginning in his upper chest, blurred features, huge jowls, and a fog in his eyes. This was the period of late-night desperate calls to former friends all over the country, full of paranoid and delusional remarks.

The publisher Barney Rosset told me that when Kerouac was living in Northport, Long Island, in the mid-1960s, he would call him in South-hampton railing ferociously about the Jewish New York publishers who would no longer give him a chance. The grotesque awkwardness was emphasized by a ranting vehemence of poisoned feeling, a terrible jeering turbulence evident in one of his last public appearances of the William Buckley television program *Firing Line.* Kerouac was hopelessly drunk in full view of millions of television viewers, helpless in the vise of a sudden celebrity that had flattened him like an oak in an avalanche, and had forgotten him almost as quickly. No wonder that in a poem he compared fame to a dirty newspaper blowing down Bleecker Street. In all fairness, however, some of the element of diatribe and denunciation in Kerouac's last years is the expression of a fool/jerk role that both he and Allen Ginsberg had assumed as a sort of protective disguise in the 1960s when they both began to be so celebrated.

Any "role" or persona, however, can shape personality. The novelist Russell Banks, in an interview in *The Paris Review,* remembered a visit Kerouac made a year before his death. Kerouac appeared with a troupe of some forty followers he had collected in a bar, among them three Micmac Indians from Quebec, who were driving him to Florida to join his mother. Kerouac had received an advance for what would be his last novel, *Vanity of Duluoz,* and was spending it "like a sailor on leave." Kerouac "brought with him a disruptiveness and wild disorder, and moments of brilliance, too," Banks recalled, and could switch personas at will. He could rant one moment and could then offer twenty-minute recitations of William Blake or Hoagy Carmichael song lyrics. For Banks, the rough personalism and expansiveness in Kerouac's work were still present in the man, even though a tortured sadness was dominant.

Like Scott Fitzgerald's, this was one of the saddest American stories. Fitzgerald could not control his drinking, and also died before he was fifty. The saddest element in Kerouac's story was his obstinate denial of his paternity of his daughter, Jan, who had been conceived in 1951 by Joan Haverty, Kerouac's second wife, after the marathon spurt that resulted in *On the Road*. Joyce Johnson, in her exquisite memoir *Minor Characters*, remembers how in 1957 Kerouac had taken a photograph of Jan out of his wallet, arguing that Joan had been sleeping with other men while they were together, and that he was certain he was not Jan's father.

Was Kerouac valuing his literary creation more than the human? Was this an illustration of an artistic irresponsibility that gives some creative souls the space in which to do their work in the first place? If so, how come Kerouac could never separate himself from the mother to whom he was so hopelessly, and perhaps in a figurative sense umbilically, attached?

Joyce Johnson noticed an unmistakable resemblance—a saturnine intensity in the eyes, perhaps?—and that Kerouac had carefully replaced the photograph in his wallet. For Johnson, it was not a simple question of "wrong and blame, but of terrible loss and sorrow." That loss and sorrow, however, seems so central in Kerouac's story, and the affirmations of so many of his emboldened characters seem a willful compensation for it. And on another level, the denial and ultimate abandonment of Jan seem to confirm Burroughs's shrewd observation that Kerouac was "an expert in unconscious sabotage."

There is little question that at the end of his life Kerouac was merely the shell of the man he had been when he did his best writing. Jan Kerouac has written an account of her second and final visit to her father in November 1967 in Lowell. Only fifteen, pregnant, bruised and battered by her promiscuous use of drugs like LSD and heroin, on her way to Mexico with her boyfriend, she was in some ways a caricature of the excess and restless questing of so many of Kerouac's characters. He sat in a rocking chair with a fifth of whiskey a foot away from a television watching *The Beverly Hillbillies* and could barely look at her.

But life is a series of passages. We change as we age, some of us evolve, others devolve and disintegrate. At this point, Kerouac was ruined, a different person from the man who once discovered the power and beauty of America in a fast car driven by Neal Cassady. To judge his life, or especially what he had written as a young novelist in his prime, by the standards of what he said in his final decade of despair seems fraudulently unfair, an ironic deployment of the sort of facile moralizing Kerouac deliberately excluded from the best of his fiction.

IX   Canonization

I remember reading Kerouac's last book, *Vanity of Duluoz,* when it appeared in 1968. I had been asked to review it for a liberal magazine called *The Catholic World,* and I was disturbed by a bloated rhetoric— what Yeats once defined as "the will trying to do the work of the imagination." The novel is marred by a flailing anger released without a cohering narrative to sustain it. I said then that the novel presented a "figure in flight, retreating without quite understanding the reasons for running. And it does this with a sense of diffusion, of transiency, of experiences rushing by without focus or real development."

That was probably the brief period of nadir of Kerouac's reputation. Kerouac once said, in a letter to Neal Cassady, that he had inherited the "curse of Melville." When Melville visited Hawthorne in London on his pilgrimage to Jerusalem, Hawthorne so perceptively understood that Melville had chosen a sort of spiritual annihilation because of the public's rejection of *Moby-Dick.*

Like Poe's, Melville's reputation was posthumous, created by his biographer, Raymond Weaver, who incidentally was one of Kerouac's favorite teachers at Columbia and who introduced him to gnosticism. Three years after Kerouac's early death in 1969, Joyce Johnson persuaded the McGraw-Hill trade department to publish *Visions of Cody* for an advance of $10,000. When I read it I felt the presence of a genuine masterpiece, which no one had wanted to print in its fullness during Kerouac's lifetime because it was just too experimental, too improvisatory, too free, at times too close to the edge of not even communicating except with the indirection of poetry.

In the 1970s, Kerouac's audience began to grow as more and more young people began to read *On the Road* as a kind of cultural bible. While some of them were entranced by the rhythmic power of the prose, others were attracted by Kerouac's depiction of his magnetic friend Neal Cassady, who, as Lawrence Ferlinghetti once observed, "will always be young and loud in our hearts." Kerouac's popularity was both inevitable and ironic, resulting from the admiration of a counterculture Kerouac had scorned, labeled as Communist, and castigated in his final years.

Ann Charters's editions of the first volume of Kerouac's letters and *The Portable Jack Kerouac* in 1995 were widely reviewed. The attention was a sign of impending canonical status, even though the American academic world largely still does not seem to fully appreciate Kerouac's importance for American literature. In some part, this may be a matter of pedigree—and most academicians are unaware that Kerouac was helped by two important critics, Alfred Kazin, who suggested to Robert Giroux, then an editor at Harcourt Brace, that he publish Kerouac's first novel, *The Town and the City*, and Malcolm Cowley, who recommended to Viking that it publish *On the Road* and helped sections of it appear earlier to further that process.

The exceptions to this academic myopia are growing, however. Ann Douglas, who teaches at Columbia University, reviewing *Selected Letters: 1940–1956* in the *New York Times Book Review*, observed that "Kerouac's work represents the most extensive experiment in language and literary form undertaken by an American writer of his generation."

Charters has edited a second volume of the letters, Viking is publishing Kerouac's notebooks, eventually the early writing will be released, and the biographical attempts to understand him will continue. But the publication by Viking of *Some of the Dharma* in 1997 is probably as significant as all of the above.

Some of the Dharma is a series of notebook entries—poems, prayers, journal notations, letters, and commentaries—in which Kerouac entered his most private thoughts about Buddhism. This was the way Kerouac had chosen to weather his deepest despair from 1954 through 1955, when it did not seem that *On the Road* would be published, in large part because of Kerouac's uncompromising stand on revision.

Written during a period when he felt he had done the best writing in America, even though most of it seemed unpublishable, it clarifies his use of Buddhism as a psychic balance for what he realized was an American lust to consume the universe. Christianity, he argued in *Some of the Dharma*, was a "theodicy," a religion about God, while Buddhism was a "cosmodicy," a religion about the universe.

Kerouac's Buddhism was always pragmatically accommodated to his special road, the journey into America he imagined for his fellow travelers. At one point he explained it as a "deviceless dharma" and offered the following advice:

> Get an old panel truck for $95 and be your own Monastery in it, parking in the open desert and on wild seacoasts . . . and in the mountains and on the outskirts of Mexican villages and in the great woods north and south—carrying mattress, food, books, typewriter, camping equipment, brakeman's lantern, and the determination to keep rolling and keep on the path of purity.

Like Thoreau's, Kerouac's Buddhism was an American hybrid, an amalgam of self-sufficiency, absorption in the beauty of nature, and the pursuit of a nonmaterialist path. As an artist, Kerouac was aware that Buddhism tends to be as authoritarian as any institutionalized religious practice that narrows an individual's sense of inquiry and options.

The "purity" of Kerouac's own Buddhist aspirations was to some extent compromised by his Catholic conditioning and his role as a writer. The state of blissfully undifferentiated being that the Buddhist seeks offers little support for the writer who depends on such finite discrimina-tions. The Buddhist suspects any form of desire and ego as intensely as a writer like Kerouac depends on passion and the projection of his own life as heroic myth. And while Kerouac could intellectually accept the proposi-tion that everything is emptiness, as he observed the loss of his own power to write, his awareness of own personal void grew larger and more threat-ening, and he needed the alcohol to fill the hole.

In *Some of the Dharma*, he is aware of the danger of his drinking and in a note observed that it was just as much a way of abandoning others as oneself. Much earlier, Burroughs had warned him in a letter from Mexico that "Buddhism was psychic junk," and on August 24, 1954, Kerouac admitted that for him the real danger of Buddhist belief was that it dead-ened his feelings and silenced his "unspoken despair."

Ultimately, *Some of the Dharma* will be mined by scholars for its auto-biographical revelations. He confesses, for example, that his "mother's happiness is the only thing that really matters to me" and that he cannot renounce the world as completely as he would like to "until I have done serving my mother, who brought me into the world."

X   *Casualties*

Ultimately, American culture has the capacity to co-opt its most dissident voices, to use art to sell anything from soap to submarines, to transform Walden Pond into a Disneyland outpost. As an artist, Kerouac was transgres-sive. Henry Miller praised a quality of "delectable madness" in Kerouac, which Allen Ginsberg qualified as "devotional" in the dream account that I cite as the epigraph to this chapter. The danger for Kerouac's critics and biog-raphers is the oversimplification of pathography, or the effort to sublimate the "madness" in the name of a homogenized middle-class respectability.

The unsophisticated critic blames for the sake of sensation, only too willing to warp the complexity of a whole life for a facile polemic. The most recent charge is Ellis Amburn's fuzzy, undocumented notion that Kerouac's career as a novelist foundered on the shoals of a repressed homoeroticism.

We all have to live with contradiction and inconsistency, artists even more than most. More than any American writer of his time, Kerouac lived the paradox of the observer entranced by motion, a man whose mind was always in flux. In his writing, Kerouac could exult, exalt, celebrate joy, and descend into dark gloom and despair. In his personal relationships, Kerouac was capable of great sweetness, charm, and consideration as well as a flaming redneck rudeness, a raw, impulsive vigor some people found alarming.

Kerouac hated hitchhiking, didn't drive, and relied on the Greyhound bus for voyages that inevitably ended at his mother's hearth. Such notions are hardly consonant with the myth of the reckless wanderer that Kerouac sustained so marvelously in his fiction, but they are reminders of the nuances of personality and intention that are part of the fabric of any major creative figure in any era. While he was able so seismically to record major changes in American life, he was not nearly as resilient or responsive as some of the characters he invented. His brief life ended as one of the great casualties of American literature.

```
              ^

              ^

              ^

              ^

              ^

              ^

<   <   <   <   <   O   >   >   >   >   >   >   >   >   >   >   >   >

              O

              O

              O

              *

          *       *

        *     *     *

      *     *     *     *

    *     *     *     *     *
```

Joyce Johnson with Daphne at home, 1997.

I met Joyce Johnson in 1971 upon hearing that Jack Kerouac's *Visions of Cody* would be published by McGraw-Hill. I had read James Laughlin's 1959 abridged version and felt its nascent power. Curious about why the work had never been issued in its entirety, I wondered why it was appearing posthumously.

I intended to review *Visions of Cody* for *Partisan Review* as part of a reconsideration of Kerouac. Meeting Joyce in her office at McGraw-Hill, I did not resemble anything Beat—I was wearing a very sharp, hand-tailored, three-piece suit that my wife had bought me, not the informal sort of red-and-black-checked lumberjack shirt Kerouac favored.

Joyce hoped to bring as much of Kerouac back into print as she could. When I asked her why, her response, so modestly understated but so firm, was that it was the repayment of a debt.

Soon, she arranged a contract for *Naked Angels*. Fortunately, I had found an editor who could really help, who knew her subject intimately because she had lived it. This was long before she wrote *Minor Characters,* her account of a love affair with Kerouac in 1957, the year *On the Road* appeared, but she had recollections, letters from Jack Kerouac to share, lots of solid leads, and good advice.

We had one impasse. When I finished a first draft, Joyce found some of the prose too impassioned. She argued that *Naked Angels* would be more convincing if my style was plainer, less heated, if I refrained from images and rhythms best reserved for a novel. I was upset. When I received a National Endowment fellowship in 1974, I fled to Oaxaca for a year and tried to improve my book.

I don't know whether I resolved this stylistic difference to Joyce's satisfaction. In the end, I deposited the manuscript and escaped again, this time to Southeast Asia with Mellon, who was awarded a grant from *National Geographic* in 1975. I left Joyce with the painstaking matter of negotiating permissions, something only a really dedicated editor would do.

We remained in touch. I interviewed Joyce for the Kerouac film I was working on in Boulder during the summer of 1982. Joyce visited us in Paris the following winter and encouraged me to begin my biography of Ezra Pound.

Recently, at the Roosevelt Center in Middelburg, Holland, Joyce spoke eloquently on what it meant to be a woman among the Beats in the 1950s. Again, I was moved by her uncomplaining understanding, her compassion, and her calm determination to make her point of view prevail.

Hunter S. Thompson, NYU Beat Conference, 1994.

Our most vitriolic and maverick journalist since H. L. Mencken, Thompson has used his bizarre wit to flog the myth of the American Dream, its platitudes and false pieties. Thompson conceived the title of his best-known book, *Fear and Loathing in Las Vegas,* on November 22, 1963, the day of Kennedy's assassination. Both his fear of governmental control and his loathing for mindless consumerism have colored his blend of comic despair, parody, hyperbolic irritation, and invective.

Inspired by Faulkner's comment that the best fiction is closer to truth than journalism, he based his controversial gonzo style, highly impressionistic, subjective without the pretense of a feigned objectivity, on a bit of South Boston slang—a gonzo is the last man standing after a drinking spree. He began his cultural interpretation of the 1960s in articles for *The Nation* on the Hell's Angels motorcycle club, on the Berkeley Free Speech Movement, and on Malcolm X and Ken Kesey.

As a young man, Thompson saw himself as a "beatnik," to use the San Francisco columnist Herb Caen's play on "Sputnik." In *The Proud Highway,* his collection of letters, Thompson has described how in the fall of 1958, during a period when he was studying at Columbia University, he was drinking one night in the West End bar. Along with hundreds of others in the bar, he saw Kerouac interviewed by John Wingate on television. Kerouac, he felt, was our national troubador, the Bob Dylan of his day.

Influenced by *On the Road,* Thompson was as irreverent and rowdy as any of its characters. Once, in the spring of 1959, when Gregory Corso was reading at The Living Theatre with Kerouac, who was red-faced, drunk, and slumped under the speakers' table, Thompson began kicking empty cans of beer down the aisle like hockey pucks. Corso was enormously disturbed and ended up shouting.

In December 1965, Ken Kesey invited Allen Ginsberg to meet the Hell's Angels at a party at his house in La Honda, California. With his usual lack of sentimentality, Thompson described the meeting between the Beats and the leather boys as a defining moment of countercultural miscalculation. Kesey, in orange jacket and headphones, was the MC at his own home circus. He was on a Peter Pan trip, Thompson concluded, showing films on a trampoline screen with the Rolling Stones blasting through speakers planted all over the redwood hillside. Outside Kesey's gate were four police cars, their "red lights revolving in the leaves," a detail Ginsberg would use to end his poem commemorating the event.

Howl—which Ed Sanders compares to a tornado in his *Tales of Beatnik Glory* (1975)—appeared when Sanders was a senior in a Kansas City high school. It helped him decide to be a poet. When he read *On the Road* a year later, he dropped out of the University of Missouri and hitched to New York.

His first book, *Poem from Jail,* written on cigarette-pack paper and smuggled out of a jail cell in his shoes, was published by City Lights Books. An anarchistic pacifist, Sanders, with two friends, had been arrested in New London, Connecticut, when they tried to swim in the path of a newly launched nuclear submarine.

In 1964, Sanders rented a former kosher butcher shop on the Lower East Side of Manhattan and called it the Peace-Eye Bookstore. On a mimeograph machine, he printed thirteen issues of a legendary underground magazine with the unlikely and at the time distinctly uncommercial title *Fuck You: A Magazine of the Arts,* including work by Burroughs, Ginsberg, Corso, McClure, Mailer, and others. In a flamboyantly immodest contributor's note, Sanders identified himself as a "dopethrill psychopath" with "an Ankh symbol tatooed on his penis."

The Peace-Eye became a meeting place for poets, musicians, and social activists. In 1966 the New York City police raided it and charged Sanders with obscenity, in part because Sanders had formed a rock group known as the Fugs. The name is derived from a euphemism for a well-known four-letter word imposed on Norman Mailer by the publisher of *The Naked and the Dead,* his novel about the Second World War.

Sanders is a second-generation Beat, a student of Greek and Egyptian myth as well as the biographer of Charles Manson. He has satirized the fringe imitators of the Beat movement in some of his fiction. He printed an edition of one of Burroughs's most scabrously outrageous pieces, "Roosevelt After Inauguration," and Burroughs, Pound, Charles Olson, and Michael McClure have influenced his poetry.

In the fall of 1968 he appeared with Jack Kerouac on William Buckley's television program *Firing Line.* Incongruously, Sanders thought Kerouac was a state trooper in the elevator on the way to the studio. Actually, Kerouac was drunk and had been for days. Even more than Ferlinghetti, for example, Sanders was militantly involved in social protest, while Kerouac was basically apolitical and Dionysian. A sorry spectacle with a cup of whiskey at his side, Kerouac quipped that a cop had given him a "ticket for decay," and that the Vietnam War was merely a conspiracy to acquire American jeeps. A year later, Kerouac would die in St. Petersburg, Florida, when the blood vessels in his stomach exploded.

Jan Kerouac, New York, 1995.

In *Train Song* (1988), her second novel, Jan Kerouac describes visiting Allen Ginsberg and Peter Orlovsky at their place in Boulder during the 1982 Kerouac Conference. Discussing meditation practice with Allen, preparing a pumpkin pie in the
kitchen with Peter, she finds the visit warm and familial. But the conference deep-
ens her awareness of her father's repeated disavowal of his paternity. That denial
had become the defining principle of her life—"it soaks through the firmament of
myself," she exclaims in her novel.

Jan Kerouac's autobiographical account *Baby Driver* (1982) reveals an enormous struggle to establish self-worth in the face of such rejection. Part of her
teen years were spent wandering the streets of the Lower East Side of Manhattan,
addicted, abused, selling herself. During the horrors of that period, she managed
some fragmentary association with Ginsberg, who was unable to reach her, and
she ended up in mental hospitals and reformatories.

I spent an hour with her in Joyce Johnson's hotel room in Lowell, Massachusetts, in 1988. We were there to witness the dedication of the Kerouac Memorial,
probably the most imposing literary monument in America. Wan and sallow, Jan
was shadowy and elusive, peering uncertainly as though she were terribly near-
sighted, a ravaged, scarred figure. In so many ways she resembled her father—
the same nomadic restlessness, a similarly self-destructive reliance on drugs, a
desperate need to write down a life story as a justification. Then there was the
uncanny physical resemblance: the dark glow in the eyes, the slightly protruding
lower lip, the squarely jutting jaw.

In 1994 she sued her father's estate, claiming that she had been deprived,
that there had been a forged will. In a final macabre act of desperation, she tried
to have her father's grave moved from Lowell. Like her father, she died before she
was fifty. In Jan's case her kidneys and spleen failed.

Mellon's photograph evokes the gamy playfulness in Jan's fiction, a counter-
feit pose for the pain she endured. The flag suggests another aspect of her father.
When the Merry Pranksters drove to New York in 1964, Neal Cassady tried to
drape an American flag over Jack Kerouac's shoulders, a prankster gesture that
Kerouac repudiated and condemned.

Painter and sometime saxophone player Larry Rivers had an early affinity for the Beat Generation and published a story, "The Addicts," in *Neurotica,* an early Beat publication, in 1950.

In the late 1940s, Rivers lived on West Twenty-first Street in Manhattan in a $4-a-week rooming house called the Penzone. Bill Cannastra, one of the firebrand catalysts of the Beat Generation, lived a bit farther to the west. Kerouac was a friend of Cannastra's who used to throw wild parties in his loft, which is where Rivers met Kerouac and Ginsberg.

All during the 1950s, Kerouac, Ginsberg, and Rivers were habitues of the Cedar Tavern and the San Remo, two bars accommodating the group Kerouac called the subterraneans. Rivers would see Kerouac at a downtown jazz bar called the Five Spot, and in 1957–58, Rivers organized weekly jazz-poetry sessions there. Later, Rivers would complete a series of pencil drawings illustrating Kerouac's *Lonesome Traveler*.

In 1959, Rivers played Neal Cassady in Robert Frank's film *Pull My Daisy*. "I never understood this goofy little masterpiece as it was being filmed," Rivers claims in his autobiography, *What Did I Do?* "But it was pleasurable playing the part of a stoned train conductor carrying a kerosene lamp in the company of such Beat luminaries."

Another Beat nexus was The Living Theatre, on Fourteenth Street and Sixth Avenue, which fomented a sense of artistic community by involving collaborations with artists such as John Cage, Merce Cunningham, and Robert Rauschenberg and poets like John Ashbery and Frank O'Hara, two of Rivers's closest friends. Rivers read his own poems at The Living Theatre one night, sharing the stage with Ray Bremser in dark sunglasses, Ginsberg, and LeRoi Jones.

Jones, a black poet, and his Jewish wife, Hettie Cohen, edited an important magazine, *Yugen,* and ran the Totem Press, both open resources for Beat writers. Rivers created the sets for two of Jones's plays, *The Slave* and *The Toilet,* works of violent hatred written in the mid-1960s as Jones was reconceiving his own identity as a writer, ending his marriage, and becoming the black nationalist Amiri Baraka.

Mellon's photograph was taken at the Whitney Museum Beat Retrospective, where Rivers's paintings were displayed with two of Julian Beck's, other paintings by Michael McClure, Lawrence Ferlinghetti, and Jack Micheline, collages by Burroughs, and photographs by Ginsberg.

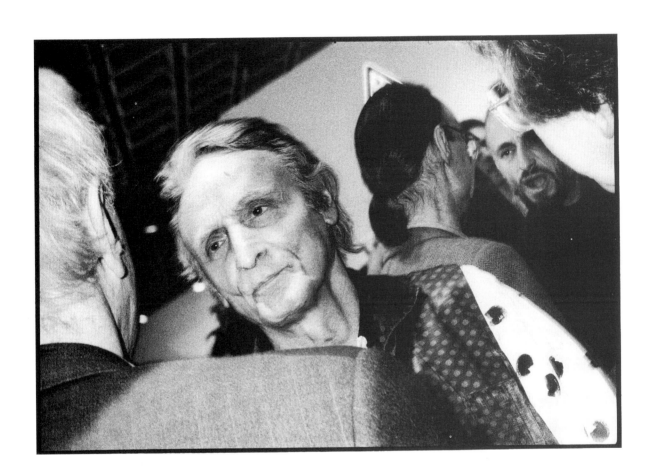

Close cousins of the Beats, The Living Theatre was the most radical, innovative American theatrical troupe during the 1950s and 1960s. It had been founded by Judith Malina and her late husband, Julian Beck, in 1947.

Beck met Kerouac at Horace Mann, an elite preparatory school in upper New York City, where in 1939–40 Kerouac was required to spend an additional high school year before beginning at Columbia University. While the Horace Mann football team utilized his speed as a running back, Kerouac wrote stories for the *Horace Mann Quarterly,* and so did Julian Beck.

A decade later, Julian and Judith began their annual ritual of huge all-night New Year's Eve celebrations. Kerouac came for the first time on the last night of 1952, bringing Ginsberg and John Clellon Holmes. In the diary Judith has been writing for half a century, she noticed how handsome Kerouac was, and that despite a sardonic edge, he seemed to be a free-flowing heroic figure.

When *Howl* appeared in 1956, Judith immediately discerned that the title poem was one of "vast significance," and she read it aloud to Julian driving up the West Side Highway in a spring snowstorm.

Up to this point, their theater had followed a gypsy path. When they were ejected from the Cherry Lane in the Village, they continued performing in their apartment, then in a loft uptown. Judith and Julian found a more permanent location in a former men's department store on Fourteenth Street and Sixth Avenue in 1958, and the Beats were welcomed as part of their extended artistic family. Carl Solomon, an escapee from Pilgrim State, briefly helped with the renovations, mostly conducted by the actors and their friends.

Many of the Beats read from The Living Theatre stage, but Ginsberg felt the closest kinship. Once he accompanied Judith and Julian to the swank St. Regis Hotel as guests of Salvador Dalí, who informed Allen that "gold is the measure of genius." Ginsberg sympathized with the pacifist protests that Judith and Julian organized, and he mythologized them in "Howl": "weeping and undressing while the sirens of Los Alamos wailed them down."

From 1990 to 1993, I researched my history of The Living Theatre in a cluttered, crowded archive that spread through Judith's apartment on the Upper West Side, coincidentally just two blocks from where I was raised.

Mellon took this photograph in our living room in the Village in 1994 when the galleys for my book appeared. Judith came downtown for her copy, and we shared a few bottles of champagne.

At nine o'clock, elated and high, we left for a theater across town where Judith was scheduled to perform in *Mysteries,* perhaps the most strenuous of all The Living Theatre productions.

Mellon and I were amazed at how quickly Judith snapped into sobriety. At sixty-eight, her stamina was striking as she groveled in anguish during the twenty-minute scene dramatizing the effects of the plague that ends the play.

The French poet Henri Michaux once declared that reading Ira Cohen was like "smoking raw nerves." I met Ira in 1975 in Kathmandu, where he was living. In a black cape, looking like a maudlin Edgar Allan Poe, he was ceremoniously seated in a rickshaw. A few weeks later, in a café on Freak Street, I heard him read part of his Stauffenberg Cycle poems, a series dedicated to Julian Beck of The Living Theatre, whom Ira called the reincarnation of Emma Goldman. Ira was coughing blood that night, his voice dissidently bohemian, an expatriate scream in the night.

Photographer and filmmaker as well as poet, from 1961 to 1965, Ira lived in Tangier, where he met Burroughs, Gysin, and Paul Bowles, and published Burroughs in an underground magazine called *Gnaoua.* My direct psychic connection to The Living Theatre, Ira brought me to Judith Malina's Upper West Side apartment in 1990 to discuss my projected history.

Harold Norse knew Julian Beck and Judith Malina when he was living in New York in 1950–51. During the period of paranoia some artists felt at the time of the Korean War, they conceived of a plan to form a settlement in an unheated farmhouse, without electricity, near Canterbury, Connecticut, a story Norse tells in his *Memoirs of a Bastard Angel.*

Norse was an early associate of the Beats. In 1944, riding the subway in New York at three a.m., Norse saw a young man in horn-rimmed glasses reciting Rimbaud in French. The young man was Allen Ginsberg, and that was the beginning of their friendship. From 1960 to 1963, Norse lived in the Beat Hotel at 9 Rue Gît-le-Coeur and consorted with Burroughs and Gysin. An example of Norse's use of the cut-up writing technique appeared in the first issue of *Gnaoua.*

Bastard Angel was the magazine Norse published in San Francisco in the early 1970s. He used work by Burroughs, Kerouac, Ginsberg, Ferlinghetti, and di Prima in his first issue, a poem by Ira Cohen in the second, and another by Gerard Malanga in the third.

I saw a lithe Gerard Malanga, poet and photographer, dance with the Velvet Underground in the 1960s. He was then collaborating on silkscreens with Andy Warhol as well as appearing in Warhol films like *Vinyl* and *Chelsea Girls*. Malanga interviewed Burroughs in 1974. Mellon met Gerard in 1983 when he interviewed her for his book *Scopophilia: The Love of Looking.*

Robert Frank on bed with camera, 1982.

In his brilliant introduction to *The Americans,* Kerouac expresses his admiration for Robert Frank, who with "agility, mystery, genius, sadness and the strange secrecy of a shadow photographed scenes that have never been seen on film."

This was high praise for an unknown photographer, who would become very well known as a result of *The Americans.* The intensely personal, poetic, and intuitively idiosyncratic photographs Frank took from 1954 to 1957 in his travels across America on two Guggenheim Fellowships appealed to Kerouac because of their emotional frankness and their fluent spontaneity. In 1958, Frank began shooting through bus windows, the photographer's equivalent of the practice Kerouac termed "sketching," working like a painter directly from experience without retouching.

In accord with the confessional and autobiographical tenor of the Beats, Frank became more interested in self-revelation in his films and photographs. As his work evolved in the 1970s, he began forming photo sequences, sometimes scratching words into the negatives or painting over images, echoes of his own search to evoke an interior life.

Mellon describes her special relationship with Robert Frank in the Rolling Stone *Book of the Beats* (Hyperion, 1999).

Robert Frank with Hunter, 1995.

From time to time I take my dog, Hunter, along with me to visit Robert. We walk the length of Bleecker Street almost to the Bowery, where Robert lives. The best time for us is in the early morning, when the light is still soft and the street hasn't yet filled with tourists. Robert doesn't much like the West Village—it's too bourgeois—but he's watching his neighborhood turn into the same thing.

Hunter loves going to Robert's, especially to clean the crumbs off his kitchen floor. You can see that Robert likes Hunter too, although he is less demonstrative with his affection. In a sense, Robert paid tribute to my canine friend by choosing to print a photograph I took of Hunter in a small book that was recently published called *Thank You* (Scalo Press, 1996).

Robert is a man on a mission and there is always something to do. Sometimes we go with Hunter to eat at The Colonial, a congenial little resto on Houston Street, or buy film or other supplies, or occasionally he takes a camera along, a new video camera perhaps, or a tiny point-and-shoot given to him by Japanese friends. The best thing for Robert is to suddenly catch an unanticipated image, and he is always on the lookout "to see if the magic is there."

—Mellon

Carl Solomon, 1994.

In his book *Mishaps, Perhaps,* Carl Solomon declared that he had lived in a generation marked by such "charlatanry, propaganda and corruption" that there was no room left for an honest man.

Like Neal Cassady, who felt Kerouac had to some extent misappropriated him, Solomon felt awkward and uneasy about being the dedicatee and in part the subject of *Howl.*

In a very clear statement in the facsimile edition of *Howl,* Ginsberg has acknowledged that when he wrote the poem in a moment of literary obscurity, he had no idea that it "would make its way around the world and proclaim a private reference to public attention."

One consequence was that Solomon was now publicly defined by Ginsberg's stereotypes. Flinging a plate of potato salad in novelist Wallace Markfield's face as a demonstration of Dadaism, for example, became a large part of Carl's social identity and a constant reminder of his own pain.

"I'm with you in Rockland / where you imitate the shade of my mother," Ginsberg exclaimed in part three of "Howl" as the tone of the poem shifts from outrage to tender empathy and solidarity. Ginsberg admitted he had used Carl's insanity and confinement as a masque of his own ambivalent feeling toward Naomi Ginsberg, his mother, who also spent years in mental institutions and whose ultimate lobotomy he had authorized.

Nevertheless, Solomon and Ginsberg remained friends for life. Totally devoted, Carl lived with his own mother in the Bronx until she died, and then in a rooming house. His great pleasure was fishing and reading, and he continued to work as a messenger.

During one of our frequent meals together, Carl complained that he had helped a friend move some books and had injured his back. Actually, it was an early sign of emphysema.

On February 26, 1994, the day of the World Trade Center bombing, Mellon accompanied Allen Ginsberg on the D train to the Bronx Veterans Hospital to visit Carl on his deathbed. Carl was getting oxygen. Allen took copious notes and some photographs, and encouraged Mellon to use her camera as well. At one point he cleaned Carl's glasses with affectionate warmth.

Then, bending over him, Allen asked Carl's forgiveness for having put him in the spotlight and making him a sensational cipher for universal suffering in "Howl."

Mellon reported that Carl was calmly surrealistic in his last hours, claiming that he was still thinking about sex though he was fading.

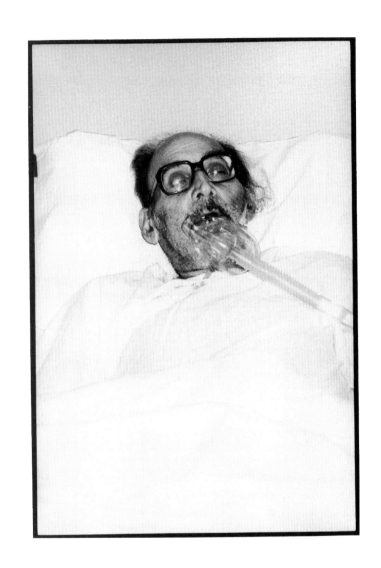

‡ ‡ ‡ ‡ ‡ ‡ ‡ ‡ ‡ ‡ ‡

Requiem for Ginsberg

Unscrew the locks from the doors!
Unscrew the doors themselves from their jambs!

—**Walt Whitman,** *"Song of Myself"*

I The Final Year

Allen Ginsberg opened the doors of poetry, of perception, of a freer life, with so cleansing a candor in such a polluted time. He was the greatest poet and teacher I've known.

I met him at his farm in Cherry Valley a quarter of a century ago. Full of scholarly curiosities and the impertinent questions of biography, I was working on *Naked Angels*—Allen's benevolent advice was to call it "Naked Humans." Allen was always a willing historian, concerned with accuracy and emotional truth. I remember spending hours in fields with Allen, talking about Burroughs and Kerouac while picking vegetables.

Ginsberg had the best understanding of Burroughs's and Kerouac's work. For Kerouac, he wrote the introduction to *Visions of Cody* and to *Pomes All Sizes*. When I did the interview with Ginsberg that was subsequently published in *Partisan Review,* half of it constituted a critical discussion of Burroughs's work. I still haven't read anything on Burroughs that surpasses its perception.

I would see him intermittently over the years, sometimes spontaneously—the key thrown from the window on Twelfth Street—but more often at the Beat gatherings that have occurred with such frequency of late. At the twenty-fifth-anniversary reading of "Howl" at Columbia University, it took Allen twenty-seven minutes to read a poem that I had heard him read years earlier at the Judson Church in twenty-two minutes.

When I asked him about the discrepancy, he explained that the breath of those long strophes was now more difficult to manage. It was my first intimation of his mortality.

The Judson Church reading occurred in the early 1960s. Ginsberg had invited the Russian delegation to the UN, who walked out in formation, twenty men in gray suits with close-cropped hair, offended by the first part of the poem. No wonder Allen was ejected from Czechoslovakia in 1965 after students crowned him King of May. The Communist puppet Czech government (like the Cubans later) claimed Ginsberg had been deported for seducing youth, but the actual reason was sedition—i.e., talking freely—the kind of talk no totalitarian system can tolerate.

Everyone knew that Allen was frail, but we were amazed at how well he could recover. At the Kerouac Conference that NYU organized in 1995, Allen had a pulmonary embolism, and his physician ordered rest. Instead, Allen spoke to several hundred people about Kerouac, as intent on spreading his word as he had been when I first interviewed him in Cherry Valley. Then he left for Europe to give a reading.

That sort of enthusiasm—the best word to characterize him, really—was the igniting spirit of his poetry. Early in 1996, I saw Kazuo Ohno, a ninety-year-old *butoh* dancer at the Japan Society. It was one of the most astonishing dance performances I've ever seen, one that defied all the expectations associated with aging and indeed death itself. After the ovation, as the audience was filing out of the auditorium, Allen remained in his seat, furiously writing in a little notebook. He continued until long after everyone had left, his diamond intensity as concentrated as Ohno's.

In the fall of 1996, at Gary Snyder's reading on Union Square, Allen's skin looked extremely sallow—an orange hue—and when he kissed me I thought it would be the final time.

On February 16, 1997, Mellon went to a morning teaching by Gelek Rinpoche, Allen's Buddhist guide, at the Jewel Heart Center in the American Thread building and sat next to Allen. When she returned home, she told me Allen looked like rigor mortis. This was unusual, because Allen—

who questioned reincarnation—was sometimes rebellious with the Buddhists, and capable of asking impossible questions.

I saw him the following night, on February 17, at the Carnegie Hall benefit for the Tibetans, and he was just sublime. Backed by Michael Stipe and Billy Corgan, he sang "Put Down Your Cigarette Rag" and the "Ballad of the Skeletons." That mordant eighteenth-century homiletic encapsulated his lifelong condemnation of what he called Moloch in "Howl," or what Burroughs called the "Control Forces"—corporate oligarchy, lobbyists, and Big Government.

For me it was the essence of what I had always seen in Allen, what he described as bhakti yoga, the pure delight of salvation by singing. The result was transcendental—which is why he was our Whitman—rhapsodic and ecstatic.

II   The Final O

Early in the morning of April 4, 1997, Mellon's birthday, I had a peculiar dream. I was eating lunch with Carl Solomon in a greasy-spoon diner, the kind Carl favored, located on the second floor of a building near Washington Square. Carl finished his tomato soup, coughed loudly, and excused himself to go the men's room.

Turning my head, I noticed Allen Ginsberg in a worn gray suit near the cashier's register, framed in the doorway and exiting. I rose to greet him and followed him through the door onto a stairway landing. Lots of people were moving up and down the dark, narrow stairway. I saw Allen moving up, rounding the corner in a spot of light at the top of the landing above. He did not hear when I called to him, but continued his ascent.

I returned to my table, and the waiter approached to inform me in a matter-of-fact manner that my table companion—meaning Carl—had dropped dead while in the men's room.

I woke from the dream to relate it to Mellon, realizing dimly that this was hardly the way to begin a birthday, but the load seemed too heavy not to be shared. Relating the dream was momentarily confusing because Carl had actually died in 1994, a few years earlier.

Forty-five minutes later, doing yoga, we heard announced on National Public Radio that Allen had terminal liver cancer. What we did not know was that he had been released by Beth Israel Hospital a few days earlier, conveyed in a wheelchair by his assistant Bob Rosenthal three blocks through the streets to his new loft in the painter Larry Rivers's building on Fourteenth Street.

On April 4, Allen took a bad turn—possibly he suffered a stroke. Many friends were with him, including Peter Orlovsky, his lover for over three decades, and Gregory Corso, Patti Smith, and Larry Rivers from the loft above, wandering about in pink-white-and-blue-striped pajamas.

Ginsberg's friend Rosebud Pettet described his final hours in the tribute at St. Mark's Church. Allen, in a Jewel Heart T-shirt, lay in a narrow bed, under a photograph of Whitman. His breathing was extremely labored; he was really gulping for air, although there were tubes from his nostrils attached to a portable oxygen tank.

Incense mingled with the scent of flowers. A group of Tibetan monks led by Gelek Rinpoche, his instructor in dying, were chanting and praying. At two-fifteen on the morning of April 5, illuminated eerily by a single low light, Allen suffered a convulsion. Peter Orlovsky then kissed his head, saying, "Goodbye, darling."

Rosebud Pettet noticed a tremor, and then, as she described it,

> slowly, impossibly, he began to raise his head. He weakly rose until he was sitting almost upright, and his left arm lifted and extended. Then his eyes opened very slowly and very wide. The pupils were wildly dilated. I thought I saw a look of confusion or bewilderment. His head began to turn very slowly and his eyes seemed to glance around him, gazing on each of us in turn. His eyes were so deep, so dark, but Bob Rosenthal said that they were empty of sight. His mouth opened, and we all heard as he seemed to struggle to say something, but only a low soft sound,

a weak "Aaah" came from him. Then his eyes began to close and he sank back onto the pillow. He continued, then, to struggle through a few more gasping breaths, and his mouth fell open in an O.

III   The Candor Man

Unlike most poets who begin so brilliantly, Ginsberg never burned himself out, but continued to create remarkable poetry. After his death, in what amounted to a last-page editorial in the *New York Times Book Review,* its editor, Charles McGrath, asserted that Ginsberg had failed to match the genius of *Howl* and *Kaddish.* This has been the perennial establishment view of Ginsberg, a cliché of criticism that has been routinely applied to great poets from Wordsworth to Whitman. The attitude is condescendingly wrong, as silly as claiming Whitman's only great poem was "Song of Myself." Ginsberg's imagination as a poet was always at the borders and beyond, inventing the new. If you don't share this belief, consult Helen Vendler, or read the tribute she contributed to *The New Yorker* of November 6, 1996, six months before his death.

Most of the critics haven't quite understood Ginsberg's humor—to call it surrealism is a misunderstanding—and they have had a continuing problem with what John Hollander once criticized as Allen's decorum. The feeble argument that Ginsberg is more imposing as a cultural force than as a poet only marginalizes poetry more than need be. "Literature is news that stays news," Ezra Pound once declared, and besides a certain element of bombast in Pound's pronouncements on poetry is often a brilliant truth.

"I would call that man poet," Henry Miller wrote, "who is capable of profoundly altering the world." Ginsberg changed the world of poetry with the overwhelming excess of *Howl.* He put "his queer shoulder to the wheel," as he promised in his poem "America," to do his best to better the world. Ginsberg had less fear—of convention or the state—than any other man I've known. Allen believed that things could change, that no authority was absolute, and in the service of such notions he was a main organizer of the protests against the Vietnam War and of what is called the "counterculture." This was a persistent commitment, so, for example, on July 14, 1978, he sat meditating with Peter Orlovsky and three young women on the railroad tracks in Rocky Flats, Colorado, impeding the progress of a train transporting fissionable materials.

Our principal spokesman for candor and spontaneity in an age of secrecy and denial, he offered his remarks on censorship or psychedelics to congressional committees or *People* magazine. But Allen's ambition was not only political: because he believed in poetry, he supported a number of poets, accommodating some of them and their families at Cherry Valley. With his "palsied lip," as he put it in a poem on teaching at Brooklyn College, he was nevertheless the most passionate reader of poetry since Dylan Thomas, a fact some academicians still suspect as much as his capacity to fill a big room almost anywhere in this large country with those eager to hear him. It is no wonder that no other poet in our times has been so memorialized, in Brooklyn, Berlin, Barcelona, and Calcutta, in San Francisco and L.A., in Central Park and City Island, in the Cathedral of St. John the Divine and in Times Square.

Ginsberg was always able to Make It New, as Pound had urged, and to make his poetry relevant to our general spiritual needs. Both Pound and Ginsberg had the rare capacity to be both avant-garde and Old Master simultaneously. I find it so charming that in Venice in 1965 Ginsberg chose to play Bob Dylan and the Beatles for Pound, then seventy-nine and locked in his decade of silence, because he felt the older poet should hear the new sounds.

Ginsberg jammed with Dylan and with John Lennon, the way Kerouac had with Lester Young, because a great poet, as Pound had taught, first of all was a musician.

"When the mode of the music changes," Allen once told me, loosely paraphrasing Pythagoras, "the walls of the city shake." And his life was spent shaking those walls with his own music, beginning with the Blake that he loved, put to song, and recorded. Many musicians—from Lou Reed to Patti Smith—sang or spoke at the St. Mark's Church memorial, which lasted for five hours with a line around the block despite the pouring rain.

Our Zeitgeist poet in a particularly dark time, Allen Ginsberg was the main singer of our generation. The songs he sang for us will continue to be sung as long as we have the voice and the heart to sing them.

Allen and Mellon on the D train, N.Y.C., 1994.

I did this self-portrait with Allen when we went to visit Carl Solomon as he lay dying in the Bronx. Underneath his brown down jacket, Allen wore a navy blue Christian Dior blazer that he had bought at the Salvation Army in Cincinnati for nine dollars. In his City Lights book bag, a gray-and-red-striped tie seemed to appear and disappear like a dancing snake.

Throughout the day, Allen repeated things that he learned from his Tibetan Buddhist teacher, Gelek Rinpoche. Over and over he said, "my teacher told me that death is neither good nor bad. It just is," as if he was trying to convince himself that this was really true. He sounded like a schoolboy studiously memorizing his lesson.

I reminded him that the first time I met him he urged me to meditate. "How presumptuous of me," he replied.

"Has it helped you?" I ask.

"I've been doing meditation for twenty years but it hasn't really helped, except to let me know when I am angry."

Even so, until the end of his life Allen was profoundly involved with Tibetan Buddhism.

—Mellon

Learning from the Beats:

A Few Notes on Pedagogy

Donkeys, camels, llamas rickshaws, carts of merchandise pushed by straining boys, eyes protruding like strangled tongues—throbbing red with animal hate. Herds of sheep and goats and long-horned cattle pass between the students and the lecture platform. The students sit around on rusty park benches, limestone blocks, outhouse seats, packing crates, oil drums, stumps, dusty leather hassacks, mouldy gym mats. They wear levis-jellabas . . . hose and doublet—drink corn from mason jars, coffee from tin cans, smoke gage (marijuana) in cigarettes made of wrapping paper and lottery tickets . . . shoot junk with a safety pin and dropper, study racing forms, comic books, Mayan codices. . . .

—William Burroughs,
"Campus of Interzone University," *Naked Lunch*

Though longevity is more a matter of luck than virtue, my guess is that I've been consistently teaching Beat writing longer than anyone else in the American academy. Some of my colleagues have accused me of inventing the subject rather than discovering it as a student in the late 1950s by reading Al Aronowitz's *New York Post* columns and attending a few poetry readings at George Preston's Artists Studio on the Lower East Side of Manhattan.

Of course, anyone employed in a university understands that envy is its debilitating disease. I've had to endure the dour condescension of colleagues who reminded me that I was hired to teach Henry James. And I have tried to do that, along with Conrad, Joyce, Fitzgerald, and a host of other personal favorites. But I have made the Beats a missionary effort, and I estimate that in my classrooms I've introduced over five thousand students to *On the Road*, and almost as many to *Howl* or *Naked Lunch*.

I had begun teaching the Beats at every opportunity as early as 1970. I have always believed in the right to form my own syllabus, that professional obligations could not preclude the civil liberty of free speech, and that whatever a teacher was passionate about would ultimately be much more valuable than any doctrinaire program.

In freshman English I would use *On the Road, Howl*, and Gary Snyder (the Lannam Foundation 1989 video of Snyder discussing his poems with students is quite useful), and I would conclude a course called The American Dream with *Naked Lunch*. My Introduction to Poetry course began with Allen Ginsberg singing Blake songs (*Holy Soul Jelly Roll* on Rhino Records) and was disproportionately weighted with Beat poetry. I used Kerouac and Burroughs in introductory fiction courses, and in a more advanced class called Aspects of Fiction. In those early days, for drama and authenticity, I would incorporate taped interviews I had done with Burroughs and with Ginsberg.

I was on sabbatical in Southeast Asia in the spring of 1976 when *Naked Angels* was printed—I read the galleys in Bangkok—and I spoke about the Beats at university campuses in Malaysia, Indonesia, Thailand, and India. My lectures were received with a polite, bland indifference, which I supposed was more due to linguistic than cultural differences. I do remember that in Ching Mai, in northern Thailand, a small bird swept through the room after my talk comparing the Beats to their transcendentalist ancestors, and I regarded it as an annunciation of sorts. I was flattered, also, when the dean of the university offered me a job at $100 a month, which went pretty far then.

I returned to Queens College, however. I proposed a course on the Beats, but the proposal seemed mired in a committee with more important curriculum matters to consider. The borough of Queens is distinguished for having more space devoted to cemeteries than any other metropolitan region, so I realized I would probably have to teach the Beats elsewhere first.

I taught my first version of a Beat class in 1976 at the New School for Social Research in Manhattan. Of the twenty-three students who registered, only a smattering had any familiarity with the Beats, and only sixteen of them completed the course. I was an enthusiast seeking converts. They were mostly diffident youngsters with a desire for a spoonful of culture, and the Beats may have been too raw to be considered cool.

A generous colleague, Wendy Martin, had heard that Rutgers wanted someone to teach a course in the Beats and recommended me. At Douglas College, I had a huge class equipped with a graduate student to correct papers, and as the visiting lecturer who drove the New Jersey Turnpike twice a week to speak about *The Wild Boys* or *Lonesome Traveler* to the future mainstream of New Jersey, I again felt more than a bit out of place. While I found that many of my students were more interested in the Beats than in *Pilgrim's Progress* or *Paradise Lost*, the interest was vicarious and sensational—more like reading about movie stars in *Vanity Fair* than using literature as an opportunity to reconsider their own lives. I still believe this is one of the dangers in any course about romantic contemporaries.

Word of the success of my Rutgers class may have opened the door to teaching a Beat class at Queens College, and many of the younger members of my department were willing to support such a course. During the 1980s I offered it to day students, in the honors program (in which the students could choose their own course, and they kept choosing the Beats, much to the consternation of some of my colleagues), to evening students, to off-campus adult education groups, and on the graduate level. Generally, the response was enthusiastic, the students feeling that they were getting an entry into the culture rarely afforded in university classrooms. Most of these students were in my class out of volition rather than obligation, and they felt a generational identification. Neither the mobility of the characters in *On the Road* nor the hallucinogenic quality of the fantasies in *Naked Lunch* was unfamiliar to them. Since I was able to bring the writers into the classroom with film and tape, they felt an enviable immediacy unavailable, say, in a Milton course.

In 1982 I went to a grimy suburb of Paris and taught the Beats in St. Denis, a provincial outpost of the Sorbonne disfigured by neglect and graffiti. On four separate occasions in four months, I saw a young person reading *Sur la Route* on the Métro. The French students saw the Beats as heroic figures, anticipating their own generational break when they took to the streets in '68 and occupied branches of the Sorbonne. None of my French students were interested in structuralist or deconstructionist approaches to writers; they seemed only interested in revering or according cult status.

Some of my American students were more querulous. Many of them were offended by *Naked Lunch*, and by what they regarded as the gratuitous violence of certain lines in *Howl* (e.g., "who let themselves be fucked in the ass / by saintly motorcyclists, and screamed with joy,") or by more recent liberationist poems like "Please Master."

This points to a key pedagogical problem with any writers who are not in accord with the values of their times, or who presume standards or codes antithetical to the majority. Always worried by the prospect of complaining letters to the dean—David Cronenberg's Hollywood version of *Naked Lunch* makes this less a source of concern—I would warn my students in the beginning of the semester that some of the material might be objectionable, particularly to a fundamentalist perspective, that I saw the academy as a free marketplace for ideas, and that if they were nervous, they could always drop my course and transfer to a section of Victorian literature. Furthermore, if they were not in some way challenged by what they were reading, then they should consider the possibility that the work was dated, its power vitiated. At the same time, I would admit that Burroughs is capable of an icy viciousness like de Sade's, that sequences like the scene where Johnny and Mary hang each other in *Naked Lunch* can evoke a lost pagan memory of orgiastic excess practically erased by twenty centuries of Judeo-Christian conditioning.

Sometimes I felt that the charge of obscenity was raised as an excuse to avoid the genuine difficulty of much Beat writing. *Visions of Cody* and *Naked Lunch*, for example, do not present easy reading and should be appreciated in the context of postmodernism. The student who is intimidated by the late James, by Faulkner, or by Joyce will have little patience with Burroughs. I would generally ask my classes to read *Junky* as a realistic blueprint or model, and show them how many of its scenes are surrealistically distorted and represented in a parodic mode in subsequent works.

With Burroughs, the most difficult matter to communicate to my students was the nature of his comedy. The macabre nihilism of a perspective that burlesqued authority with so vicious an aftertaste seemed too pyrotechnically stunning to leave room for humor. As illustration, I would use the excremental menu in *Naked Lunch* (with its offering of clear camel piss soup and the limburger cheese cured in diabetic urine), or one of Dr. Benway's chaotic surgeries. Many of my students were only willing to accept such moments as aberration or nightmare. Often, I felt my students couldn't feel the humor because of a bathetic taste level that only accepted the television sitcom as genuine comedy. For some students, laughter could never be quite as bitter or as sardonic as it seemed for Burroughs.

I would play my tape of Burroughs reading his "Roosevelt After the Inauguration" routine in which he imagines FDR appointing a group of baboons to do his bidding on the Supreme Court, but this was often a poor strategy, since FDR was still beyond criticism in the northeast. Ultimately, to help my students see the comedy, I would use Howard Brookner's documentary film *Burroughs: The Movie*, especially the sequences when Burroughs played Dr. Benway making a bloody farce out of a surgery.

Brookner's unusual documentary with its strange footage of a mordant William Burroughs impersonating a Hungarian count, for example, reminds me of crucial dramatic opportunities for anyone studying the Beats. The most valuable is Robert Frank's short film *Pull My Daisy* (New Yorker Films), with the antics of Ginsberg and Corso and the inspired narration by Jack Kerouac. The film offers a view of the innocent bohemian origins of the Beats in conflict with the notions of propriety imposed by a visiting bishop. Frank's *The Americans* (originally published in 1958; I use the 1978 Aperture reprint) is another useful ancillary resource, both because it pictures so many of the smug complacencies of the 1950s and because of Kerouac's spirited introduction. And speaking of photographs, Ginsberg's snapshot record of his friends was published by Twelvetrees Press (Altadena, Calif.: 1990), and I would often present certain photos with commentary to my students such as the one of Kerouac on Ginsberg's Lower East Side firescape and of Julian Beck on his deathbed in 1985.

The best resource for studying Ginsberg is probably the original draft fascimile edition of *Howl*, edited by Barry Miles, in which Ginsberg accounts for the actual circumstances motivating the different lines of the poem. Allen Ginsberg was the best reader of poetry in our time, and there are several CD sets available. Note that the Rhino recording of *Howl* sounds fatigued; the rhythm is much better on the old 1959 LP when Ginsberg still had the requisite breath and stamina to read it properly (Fantasy Records).

A general resource I wish to recommend is the catalog to the 1995 Whitney Museum show *Beat Culture and the New America 1950–1965*, edited by Lisa Phillips, which demonstrates some of the more broad artistic ramifications of the whole Beat movement. Yet another fascinating catalog is *Ports of Entry: William S. Burroughs and the Arts*, prepared by Robert A. Sobieszek for the Los Angeles County Museum of Art 1996 exhibition of Burroughs's paintings. Another resource is the already imposing library of secondary sources, although, of course, considerable discrimination needs to be exercised here. While I admit that it may seem like special pleading to point to my own book, *Naked Angels* (published in paperback by Grove Press since 1986), for its historical and aesthetic contexts, I do think it really helps students in the digital age.

With Kerouac, I would sometimes use John Antonelli's flawed docudrama, *Kerouac* (now distributed by Mystic Fire Video). Even though it sentimentalizes and occasionally sensationalizes—e.g., the scene of Lucien Carr stabbing David Kammarer—it does have some valuable footage, like Kerouac's appearances on the Steve Allen and William F. Buckley shows. Since I wrote its original script and conducted all the interviews, I could speak to the question of how the writer is often betrayed by a medium over which he or she has limited control, and how the editing process ultimately shapes any film. Kerouac is available on tape or CD on the Rhino label (The Jack Kerouac Collection, 1990). I would use his haiku and his madcap talk on the history of bop.

Using Kerouac in the classroom has been easier than using Burroughs, although there still seem to be hazards. Generally, as with Fitzgerald, the surface ease and the overall accessibility prevents students from digging deeply enough with a book like *On the Road*. They tend not to see its deliberate patterning, its picaresque structure, its use of repetition, or the reappearance of the aged wandering prophet figure moaning for man, the Spenglerian "everything is collapsing" refrain, or the conventional novelistic elements like the symbolic death and rebirth passage in the hotel room near the railroad tracks in Des Moines at the beginning of the novel when Sal Paradise wakens to the reddening sun unable to remember his identity.

On the other hand, with as experimental a novel as *Visions of Cody*, students are unprepared for the complexity, the denseness of the text and its allusive quality. To help them hear the rhythm, which after all is Kerouac's greatest attribute, I play Kerouac reading the Marx Brothers fantasy from the novel on the Rhino collection. Students respond to Kerouac's unaffected voice and the warmth of his tone: it is especially important for my students, for, as I remind them, Kerouac lived in Ozone Park and Richmond Hill in Queens for over a decade, writing in his mother's kitchen. So as far as the history of the art of fiction in the borough of Queens goes, he is its most important practitioner.

I have described a number of audio and visual possibilities for teaching the Beats that have obvious advantages for students, but there is a correspondent disadvantage in the tendency of students to become more captivated by the dynamics of biography and less interested in textual matters. Given Kerouac's ability to mythologize himself and the other members of the Beat Generation, fictional event can become transposed to legend, and the student often becomes so fascinated by the romantic appeal of a Jaffy Ryder in *The Dharma Bums*, for example, that the often stagy programmatic qualities of the story are ignored. Similarly, both Burroughs and Ginsberg represent certain rebellious or liberating attitudes with great appeal to young people—to their sexuality, for example—and the notions they express can prevent students from distinguishing between the inevitable troughs or peaks in any artist's work. The expression of the attitude becomes its own justification and aesthetic priorities are waived.

Kerouac's evocative ability as a mythographer suggests another pedagogical dimension, that of literary biography. Kerouac, so far, has been unfortunate with his biographers, and of those who have already attempted to write his life, no one has been able to tell the story with real fluency. The best portraits have been drawn by John Clellon Holmes in *Nothing More to Declare* and Joyce Johnson in *Minor Characters*. Ann Charters has contributed an invaluable body of research material on Kerouac, beginning with her bibliography. Instead of any formal biography, I would recommend *Jack's Book*, an oral biography assembled by Barry Gifford and Lawrence Lee.

As far as general criticism is concerned, the Beats as a movement were greeted in the beginning with a lot of condescension, particularly from people who knew them at Columbia University, like John Hollander, Diana Trilling, and Norman Podhoretz. Some of the attacks were vindictively political in nature. Podhoretz, for example, along with his friend Irving Kristol, helped design contemporary conservatism, so it is no wonder he saw little merit in the liberationist openness of the Beats and instead pretended they were the unwashed remnants of a philistine mass culture.

Podhoretz's "The Know-Nothing Bohemians" appeared in *Partisan Review* in 1957, an enormously influential magazine at that time. Perhaps because of the infiltration of Hettie Jones, who worked at *Partisan Review* in the 1960s, and the editorial participation of Morris Dickstein in the 1970s, an attitude of rigid dismissal evolved to tolerance and even support.

Reliable criticism, however, is still hard to find. I always recommend Michael McClure's *Scratching the Beat Surface*, although McClure is an obvious partisan and his book is sometimes idiosyncratic and always quite personal. Two valuable critical collections are *On the Poetry of Allen Ginsberg*, edited by Lewis Hyde, and *William S. Burroughs at the Front*, edited by Jennie Skerl and Robin Lydenberg. As far as individual essays are concerned, I recommend Mary McCarthy and Marshall McLuhan's reviews of *Naked Lunch*, Oliver Harris's introduction to *The Letters of William S. Burroughs, 1945–59*, Henry Miller's introduction to the original paperback edition of *The Subterraneans*, and Seymour Krim's introduction to the original paperback edition of *Desolation Angels*.

The relatively impoverished state of Beat criticism is something that will be remedied in time, although the fact that as significant a poet as Gary Snyder has received almost no intelligent criticism since Thomas Parkinson's essays in *The Southern Review* in 1968 and *Journal of Modern Literature* in the winter of 1971 is distressing.

The case of Snyder suggests a further pedagogical matter that clearly affects students, and that is the balance between optimism and despair that in contemporary literature is so often tilted toward the dark side. Burroughs and Ginsberg begin as observers of a declining culture, and Kerouac's awareness of death is so keen a reminder of our mutability. ("All you do is head straight for the grave, a face just covers a skull awhile. Stretch that skull-cover and smile." *Visions of Cody*, p. 12.) To the extent that Burroughs was addicted to heroin and Kerouac to alcohol they are certainly compromised as models of how to live.

In general the Beats have been distrusted as the wild men of American literature. Snyder's work on trail crews and as seaman, Zen acolyte, and parent suggests more integrated possibilities that are reflected in the pragmatic base of his poems. Although he is Beat because of his place in the value system—his suspicion of a society that directs its resources to packaging, plastics, and mechanical responses—he seems more harmoniously centered on regaining feelings numbed by the industrial state.

In *The Dharma Bums*, Kerouac described Snyder's voice as resonant and brave, earnest and "humanly hopeful," and the best way to hear this is in Snyder's poems. I like to use two early poems from *The Back Country*, "After Work" and "Marin-An," as a contrast to Ginsberg's characteristic excessiveness. Snyder's quiet elegance, his tactile, unsentimental, almost unobstrusively muted voice, what might be called his ineffable texture, rarely calls attention to itself, or depends on a glittering imagery, and seems to pursue a Thoreauvian simplicity. The strength of the couple in "After Work" suggests a view of a self-sufficient older America, responding to natural human tools like the ax rather than the tractor, and the solidity of a woman's and man's dependence on each other and on the reliable comforts of fire and stew, garlic and wine. Snyder's unadorned insistence on the directly observable, his discovery of a grace in the natural, results in the sort of purity of intention we associate with Williams's "The Red Wheelbarrow," a paradox of affirmation despite our time of troubles.

From the viewpoint of the English department at Queens College, the Beat course had two distinct advantages: it usually had the largest registration of any course in the department when it was offered, and it attracted many nonmajors. From my viewpoint, it was not offered frequently enough, an opinion shared by students who on several occasions submitted petitions requesting the course.

In 1992, I was asked to deliver a university-wide talk for the Whitman centennial, which I called "Whitman and the Antinomian Tradition." In it I traced the connections between Whitman, the transcendentalists, figures like Pound and Henry Miller, and the Beats. This established the tradition out of which the Beats emerged. When I proposed this as a course to my colleagues at Queens College, however, it was fiercely criticized on what seemed to me to be the ironic grounds of political correctness. Even though I had included Joyce Johnson's *Minor Characters* and Leroi Jones's *The Dutchman* and *The Slave* in my syllabus, I was denounced for having organized a course in the work of white males.

I was researching my history of The Living Theatre, and I saw its founders, Julian Beck and Judith Malina, as first cousins to Ginsberg and Kerouac, friends and sympathizers in the same city at the same time. No one else in American theater had been quite as antinomian as Malina and Beck, so I fit them into a new course, called Some American Antinomians, which I was able to offer on a graduate level. I would show their fulcrum play, *The Brig* (available on Mystic Fire Video as well as *Mysteries, Paradise Now*, and Sheldon Rochlin's excellent documentary *Signals Through the Flames*). *The Brig*, a naturalistic indictment of the Marine Corps penal system, caused the infamous raid by the IRS that led to a decade of exile.

The Living Theatre had been incorporated in 1947, yet no one had told its story before the Grove Press publication of my history in 1995. This leads me to a final observation, perhaps more directed at graduate studies than undergraduate. Although both Ginsberg and Burroughs died in 1997, the Beats are not quite yet preserved in a Victorian past. The implications of the Beat story have only begun to be charted, and its artistic dimensions have not yet been fully explored. There is a clear need for analysis of Beat code figures like William Cannastra, Lucien Carr, and Herbert Huncke, and writers like John Clellon Holmes and Carl Solomon. With Holmes, for example, no one has bothered to compare *Go* to *On the Road*, its obvious source, and the comparison would tell us a lot about the perils of literary imitation. There is as yet no good biography of Ferlinghetti, and no biography of Corso or Snyder, though *Gary Snyder: Dimensions of a Life*, edited by Jon Halper, is a valuable oral biography.

Enterprising graduate students should know about the Ginsberg Deposit at Stanford University, the Neal Cassady–Kerouac correspondence at the Humanities Research Center in Austin, Texas, the Kerouac papers at the Berg Collection of the New York Public Library, and the Burroughs papers at Arizona State University.

In my work, I have focused on Ginsberg, Kerouac, and Burroughs because I believed they were the spokesmen of their generation. But the Beat tradition is much broader, as Ann Charters's *The Portable Beat Reader* and Anne Waldman's *The Beat Book* demonstrate, and the fact that Kerouac's daughter and Burroughs's son also wrote novels suggests it is a developing tradition, one that will continue into the twenty-first century.

Patti Smith at St. John the Divine Cathedral, 1998.

Patti Smith chanted Ginsberg's poem "On Cremation of Chogyam Trungpa Vidyaa-hara" while Philip Glass accompanied her on the piano at the Ginsberg tribute at St. John the Divine.

Fifty-one, widowed, the former punk poet who became a rock icon at places like Max's Kansas City and CBGB's, where Burroughs heard her sing in the 1970s, recently returned from a sixteen-year hiatus to tour with Bob Dylan and resume her public performances.

Patti Smith doesn't present a mannered facade, and she is known for her improvisational ability. With gray-streaked stringy hair, a faded Burroughs T-shirt, and jeans, Patti Smith is elemental and particularly honest. There is a primordial beatness in the raw grief she expresses in her songs, and her sound can become overwhelming, transcendent, ultimately healing.

At one point, her entire body vibrating, when words no longer seemed sufficient, she dropped to the ground and spoke through her clarinet, pointed upward as if beseeching Ginsberg's spirit.

Patti Smith has spoken of Ginsberg and Burroughs as sources of inspiration, and she was part of the group assembled at Ginsberg's bedside when he died. She attended Burroughs's funeral, and her remark that Burroughs "helped make the present possible by writing maps of territory that had previously been considered out of bounds" suggests the spreading circumference of the Beat paradigm, its influence on culture from New York to Berlin to Moscow.

Anne Waldman is a second-generation Beat, influenced by Burroughs's cut-ups and Ginsberg's legendary ability to perform his poems in public.

In one sense she can be regarded as a child of the Beat Generation, raised in Greenwich Village in the postwar period, passing Bob Dylan and Gregory Corso in the streets when she was twelve. She has commented that Corso was a sort of idol—"like Rimbaud, the epitome of the 'damned' poet, and so gorgeous!"

Waldman was introduced to the Beats by Donald Allen's Grove Press anthology, *The New American Poetry: 1945–60,* and began publishing her own work at the end of the 1960s. Ginsberg encouraged her to write longer poems as a way to more fully release her emotional energy. By then she was already directing the St. Mark's Poetry Project, a vital center in lower Manhattan.

Ferlinghetti's City Lights published Waldman's *Fast Speaking Woman* in 1975, a book in which she displayed her mastery of the rapid rhythmic urgency that has made her such a compelling reader. In 1975 she also became the codirector, with Ginsberg, of the Jack Kerouac School of Disembodied Poetics at Naropa. Established to encourage the notion of a community of artists, like the famed Black Mountain College, Naropa hosted a stream of the Beats during the late 1970s and 1980s, including Burroughs, Corso, Diane di Prima, Peter Orlovsky, Michael McClure, Amiri Baraka, and Ken Kesey. Ginsberg taught a class there almost every summer.

In 1981, Waldman introduced Ginsberg at the Columbia University reading commemorating the twenty-fifth anniversary of "Howl." She described Ginsberg's epic as a "monumental hymn to the liberation of the American spirit from postwar material-industrial paranoid doldrums and hypocritical self-imposed mind and body restraints. It is a poem of desperate dejection purged and epiphanied through outrageous confession and celebration."

On the day after Ginsberg's death, I saw her communing in the presence of the poet's body at the private ceremony at Jewel Heart, the Tibetan Buddhist center in lower Manhattan. A few weeks later I heard her at the more public five-hour memorial at St. Mark's Church.

Mellon's photograph was taken on the occasion of an even larger gathering for Ginsberg held a year after his death in the largest Gothic cathedral in the world, St. John the Divine. Even though the *New York Times* notified its readers of the wrong date, every one of the 2,500 seats were occupied.

Rainbow Family, Nacogdoches, Texas, 1990.

The most radical tendency of the counterculture of the 1960s was its uninhibited lust for freedom on all fronts. In San Francisco, the Diggers repudiated capitalist values by giving food and entertainment away for free. The Diggers began leaving San Francisco in 1967–68, becoming what was called the "Free Family Network," a series of communes in Marin County, north of San Francisco, connected by caravans of communicants who spread a dropout, back-to-the-land consciousness.

Groups like the Diggers evolved into the Rainbow Family, which organizes an annual gathering in different national forests during the first week of July, with Independence Day dedicated to a prayer vigil and celebration for world peace. Loosely bound by spiritual ties, the Rainbows are a Global Tribe with thousands

of individuals from almost every walk of life expressing a concern with ecology and the environment, a green army reconnecting with nature in a week of ritual assembly and Dionysian revelry. Everything is free—food and water, workshops, medical care and child care—and the exchange of money is not allowed.

In a participatory experience in self-government based on consensus democracy, the right to assemble is tested by federal authorities annually and has had to be established in the courts.

Mellon photographed these descendants of *On the Road* in 1990 during the twenty-first Rainbow Family Gathering at the Sam Rayburn National Forest in Nacogdoches, Texas, where five thousand people camped in the piney woods.

The Opening Divide

But you, a new brood, native, athletic, continental,
greater than before known,
Arouse! for you must justify me.

—**Walt Whitman,** *"Poets to Come"*

Literary historians have to twist their necks backward to forever focus on the past, so for them the issue of legacy can be a bit cloudy. But the death of both William S. Burroughs and Allen Ginsberg in 1997, almost at the end of a millennium, is a reminder that the Beats were our most significant movement in American literature since the Lost Generation. Every age has its confluence figures, the writers whose vision corresponds with or helps to form the defining attributes of an era, and who seem connected at a hundred points of intersection with various aspects of a culture.

When I interviewed Burroughs in "the Bunker" in 1974, he emphasized the cultural reach of the Beat movement, its potential to suggest new possibilities. He claimed that the Beats were part of a worldwide sociological shift. They questioned convention, restlessly searching for new sources of meaning in an alienated age. John Lennon's comment that the Beatles chose their enigmatic name because of the Beats is just one suggestive sign of the breadth of the Beat influence.

I agree with Burroughs's comparison of Kerouac to Fitzgerald, as a generational spokesman whose effect "is immediate, as if a generation were waiting to be written." If we could ask Kerouac to identify his legacy, he would probably reply that it is the work itself, particularly the posthumously published *Visions of Cody* and *Some of the Dharma.* He might also consider the irony of the Stonehenge in granite erected by Governor Dukakis in Lowell, Massachusetts, eight ten-foot-tall plinths, each engraved with a quotation from a Kerouac novel. Granite tends to endure, and the fact that *On the Road,* *Naked Lunch,* and *Howl* are still in print in over twenty countries is clearly compelling evidence of literary durability.

The first register of any writer's influence is usually the interest of younger writers, although the styles of most important writers are so personal as to be inimitable. Thomas Pynchon has remembered that while in the United States Navy, he wandered into a bookstore in Norfolk, Virginia, and found a copy of *Evergreen Review,* a magazine with a defined Beat slant started by Barney Rosset of Grove Press. Later, in his introduction to *Slow Learner: Early Stories* (Little, Brown, 1984), Pynchon admitted the magazine was "an eye-opener."

Another former navy man, the novelist Robert Stone, has recently recalled (*New York Times Book Review,* December 7, 1997) how at nineteen, a "bookish high school dropout," he volunteered to serve with the last of the Byrd expeditions to Antartica, a voyage that would last a year. He had two books with him, *Moby-Dick,* that epic announcement of the struggle to domesticate nature which has been so pronounced in American history, and *On the Road,* which his mother had sent him. Stone read *On the Road* in the winter of 1957, a few months after its publication, and acknowledged that the experience "floored me." Although the praise in his essay was qualified, Stone's response suggests the immediate power Kerouac's novel had for his generation.

For Hunter S. Thompson, perhaps the leading alternative journalist of our time, reading *On the Road* was a gestalt experience. His memory of the impact of Kerouac's novel appears in *The Proud Highway,* a collection of his letters: " . . . a great truth blundered out of the sky and imbedded itself in my skull. With a great thunderous clatter, a million jangled pieces of a long-scrambled puzzle fell miraculously into place."

Kerouac's influence was sweeping, and other artists from such different worlds as Bob Dylan and the film actor Robert Redford have testified to the galvanizing impact of reading him. Redford's account (*New York Times Magazine,* August 21, 1994) seems representative:

I used to drive up to San Francisco and sit in the North Beach cafés when I was a teen-ager. I lived in the San Fernando Valley, a place of used-car lots and appliance stores. When I read *On the Road* it struck me the way the movie *Rebel Without a Cause* did—like an arrow to the heart, to my own identity. That's what I felt about the Beats. I felt I was—like they were—on the edge of something, at the beginning of something, leading to something different.

Kerouac has become iconic. His appearance in the Gap advertisement wearing khakis was one, perhaps disconcerting, sign of his effect on popular culture. When Francis Ford Coppola issued an actors' call for roles in the projected film of *On the Road*, over five thousand hopeful aspirants lined the streets of midtown Manhattan for a chance at what had once been Marlon Brando's dream role.

Kerouac's influence has been multifaceted. His popularization of Buddhism, in *The Dharma Bums*, probably more than any other single work motivated an avenue of religious seeking that has deeply affected the culture and continues to do so. It is no accident that the Naropa Institute in Boulder, the first accredited Buddhist college in this country, named its literature program the Jack Kerouac School of Disembodied Poetics.

There have been so many attempts to write Kerouac's biography in the three decades since his death because Kerouac's appeal extends beyond the limits of literature. This extraliterary appeal has much to do with the sometimes moot issue of any writer's influence. Influence is usually diffused and indirect. And in a process over which writers have little control—although the self-mythologizing capacity of all the Beat writers is certainly a contributing factor here—they may be regarded as what Pound referred to as antennae, seismically predicting in their lives and works deep changes in American sensibility.

The critic Edmund Wilson, in a famous essay titled "The Wound and the Bow," saw the Greek archer Philoctetes, bitten by a poisonous snake and marooned by his fellow Greeks, as the prototype of the artist who has gained diagnostic power and insight by struggling with or overcoming disease. The medical analogy to such insight would be the immunity derived after exposure to illness. In non-Western cultures, the shaman healer often tries to absorb the patient's illness through touching. To the extent that we can be "touched" by their words, writers like Conrad or Kafka or Pound seem so related by this sort of shamanism that it indeed seems a defining characteristic of the modern literary sensibility.

This shamanistic capacity of the artist is also evident with Burroughs, whose work initially fascinated the literary cognoscenti—first the generation of Mailer, Vonnegut, and the science fiction masters like J. G. Ballard and Phillip K. Dick, then writers like Pynchon and Don DeLillo. Since Burroughs was one of the leading fictional innovators of our time, it is not surprising that his work so quickly crossed over into other aspects of culture, particularly music and film.

While it is true that Kerouac has inspired more than fifty songs by performers like Van Morrison, Paul Simon, and Tom Waits, Burroughs's impact has been even more pronounced in this sphere. Singer-poets like David Bowie, Patti Smith, Lou Reed, and Kurt Cobain began with him as an influence. Composer Philip Glass has been influenced by his cut-up methods. Rock bands such as Steely Dan, Insect Trust, and Throbbing Gristle found their names in *Naked Lunch*. His phrase "heavy metal" defined an entire school of hard rock, and much of the punk sensibility that followed seemed to emanate from Burroughs's vision of entropy and pain.

The 1995 exhibit of paintings by Ferlinghetti, McClure, Kerouac, and others organized by the Whitney Museum, the show of Burroughs's paintings and collage at the Los Angeles County Museum of Art in 1996, his collaborations with painters like Robert Rauschenberg, David Hockney, and Keith Haring, Burroughs's appearance on *Saturday Night Live* and in the film *Drugstore Cowboy*, and his image in a series of Nike ads have all been part of the boundary-crossing that has been a radical element in much postmodernist American art, whether with John Cage, the Abstract Expressionists, or The Living Theatre. The purpose of such transgressive artists is always to redefine the boundaries of art, and especially to remove artificial barriers between art and life that have been often constructed because of Victorian propriety, and the fear that leads to hierarchical and class-bound values.

With most of the Beats, this boundary-crossing has had an autobiographical motive. Burroughs's heroin addiction helped him develop a unique perspective on the sources of social power and control. Kerouac's loneliness and his piercing awareness of the mutability and transience of life left him with an enormous reserve of compassion. The terrible intensity of Ginsberg's feelings led to his Blake vision, which was the announcement of an oracular if apocalyptic view of modern life.

Ginsberg's photography and his performances as a singer-poet offer further evidence of shifting the boundaries, pushing the parameters of what seems possible for an artist. He set to music and sang many of the early poems of William Blake, and performed with Paul McCartney and Bob Dylan. He collaborated with Philip Glass on *Hydrogen Jukebox*, an opera. He continued to pursue the bop improvisational rhythms that Kerouac had first discovered listening to Lester Young, Dizzy Gillespie, and Charlie Parker in the fifties.

Howl had a shaping influence on American poetry in the fifties, changing the emphasis from the studied persona of T. S. Eliot and a musty academic formalism that had stifled American poetry to a more personal urgency. An early reflection can be seen in the poetry of Robert Lowell. *Lord Weary's Castle*, which won the Pulitzer Prize for poetry in 1947, was written in Eliot's removed idiom; *Life Studies*, the masterpiece Lowell completed after having read *Howl*, begins his confessional mode.

Howl exploded the possibilities for American poetry, but it also had an enormous effect on the culture at large. As Michael McClure has observed, it was as if an insiduous barrier had been broken, "a human voice and body had been hurled against the harsh wall of America and its supporting armies and navies and academies and institutions and ownership systems and power support bases."

What both *Howl* and *Kaddish* affirmed was the importance of what might be called the unspeakable cry—Kerouac called it the "unspeakable vision of the individual"—an emotionalism sufficiently extremist to overcome taboo and waken an apathetic people frozen in what Julian Beck of The Living Theatre called the "ice-age." Such release of raw emotion shivered the stiff upper lip of the John Wayne hero, the Cold War code of repression that was equated with masculinity.

Julian Beck's *The Life of the Theatre* and most of Ginsberg's oddly shaped books of poems, with their minimalist black-and-white covers, were published by Lawrence Ferlinghetti's City Lights Books, which had an anarchist perspective. Like Barney Rosset's Grove Press in New York, this was the kind of publisher that would eagerly consider the work of a writer who seemed unsuitable for more conventional publishers.

The success of *Howl* and of City Lights was a signaling beacon for the small press movement in America, an alternative resource that would become more widespread because of technology. A number of the fugitive Beat publications like *Beatitude, Floating Bear,* and Ed Sanders's mimeographed *Fuck You: A Magazine of the Arts* suggested new potentials for the small press movement, which resulted in what the Soviet-era Russians called *samizdat,* an underground press challenging settled establishment views with a more vital perspective.

Howl was confiscated by customs agents in San Francisco in 1956 and, along with *Naked Lunch,* had to be vindicated by judicial process before being disseminated. According to FCC regulations, it still cannot be read on the radio. The extreme language of *Howl* and the outrageous character of the sexual fantasies in *Naked Lunch*—which make Henry Miller seem like an avuncular pal—extended the notion of what was permissible in print in America, and now this is reflected even in more genteel publications like *The New Yorker.*

The public attempts at censorship of the Beats—and works like McClure's play *The Beard,* and certain predecessors such as *Lady Chatterley's Lover* and *Tropic of Cancer* need to be considered in this context as well—are a consequence of an honesty that the Beats regarded as primal, and that has affected their positions on sexual as well as political matters. The fact, for example, that Burroughs and Ginsberg never buried themselves in the homosexual closet of the fifties—Burroughs wrote *Queer* in the beginning of that decade, although it was published only much later—made them avatars of gay liberation. And the ideal of literary spontaneity that Kerouac espoused seems related philosophically to the naked needs of honesty. *Howl* anticipated a collective need for public and candid confession that became a defining attribute of the 1960s, an energy that was translated to the imperative needs of social change.

The Beats pursued a liberationist path. Since the end of the feudal period and the weakening of monarchy, this has been the perennial path of romantic individualism everywhere, an antinomian questioning of arbitrary authority in all its forms. In American literature, the most convincing spokesman for this sometimes belligerent striving for freedom has been Walt Whitman: "The attitude of great poets," he once wrote, "is to cheer up slaves and horrify despots."

Whitman's remark represents a revolutionary shift in the writer's perspective. Through the Renaissance, writers were patronized by an aristocracy whose values they praised. With the rise of the middle class in the eighteenth century, patronage became less important, though the values of an expanding business culture were of central interest to the novelist in particular.

An identification with the working classes such as you feel in Whitman's "Crossing Brooklyn Ferry" is a nineteenth-century phenomenon. Whitman introduced a new tone, a quality of swaggering, almost inebriated bravura, a militant Shelleyan romanticism, and a sometimes brazen personalism. These are all the hallmarks of Whitman's natural speech. His purpose, as he put it in "Song of Myself," was to "unscrew the locks from the doors" and then, stretching his metaphor, "the doors themselves from their jambs."

Ever audible in Whitman is a rhapsodic music, a surging rhythmic momentum. No wonder that Henry Miller called Kerouac his "blood-brother" in his introduction to *The Subterraneans*, recognizing that Kerouac was the next figure to march along Whitman's ecstatic vernacular path.

Whitman warned Americans to abandon their materialist path. Contrapuntal to this prophetic invective was Whitman's extraordinary compassion, reflected in his poems and in the hundreds of hospital visits he made in Washington, D.C., during the Civil War. Sympathy was the crucial Beat ingredient, Kerouac maintained, and it was as active in his idealization of a vagrant class, of the Denver blacks in the "lilac evening" section of *On the Road*, as in Ginsberg's anguish for the outcast and untouchable, the addicted or the insane.

Ginsberg in *The Fall of America*, along with poets like McClure and Gary Snyder (in *Earth House Hold* and poems like "Oil" and "The Trade"), gave us early warnings of ecological disaster. Ginsberg warned of the imminence of the "monolithic Surveillance State" and along with Burroughs was a leading voice questioning the technological values induced by the military-industrial complex—e.g., it is acceptable to consume cigarettes because they can be conveniently packaged, but marijuana leads to incarceration. While I cannot attribute the recent decriminalization of marijuana for medical use in California, Arizona, Nevada, and Washington to any single poem by Ginsberg or novel by Burroughs—in the way Upton Sinclair's *The Jungle* led to Theodore Roosevelt's establishment of the Food and Drug Administration—both of them contributed to a climate of reevaluation that encourages change.

Concomitantly, rap music is an evolution of the Beat sensibility. Kerouac's spontaneous talk "The History of Bop" (included in the Rhino Records four-CD Kerouac Collection) and Neal Cassady's early 1960s harangues for the Grateful Dead are early anticipations of rap, although neo-Beat figures like Lenny Bruce and Lord Buckley might be considered more direct influences.

In fact, the openness encouraged by the Beats has contributed to a general increase in the amount and character of poetry and fiction in our time. The example of *Howl* has enabled writers to base their creative expression more directly on their personal experiences without the decorous inhibitions of the past. Instead of fearing poetry as an art requiring an elite preparation, classical training, or at least an Ivy League education, poets after the Beats have been more inspired by concerns connected to common experience. And the release represented by the Beats was part of a great cultural turn from the intimidating and authoritarian intellectual climate of the 1950s to an unprecedented honesty of expression and sentiment.

The repercussions of the Beat movement and its quest for openness have had profound implications for our culture. The "rucksack revolution" Kerouac described in *On the Road* may have sold a few million Levi's jeans, but it also announced an optimism and a spirit of informality that was recognizably American. Even more important, it expressed a sense of community that cohered in the face of the isolation and alienation of an era. While this was reflected most intensely in the artistic mingling in the coffeehouse scene of the 1950s in places like North Beach in San Francisco and Greenwich Village in New York, it radiated toward the center to work against the pressures of conformity.

The so-called culture wars in the American academy stem from the attacks on the Beats in the late 1950s. Norman Podhoretz, editor of *Commentary*, one of the chief instigators of the conservative backlash, began his program with an article called "The Know-Nothing Bohemians," a slashing criticism of Kerouac and the Beats. Podhoretz obviously had his own agenda, and in his vindictive piece he attempted to prove that Kerouac couldn't write well.

Whether or not Podhoretz's opinions had more to do with jealousy than ideology, Kerouac's enormous appeal—more than three million copies of *On the Road* have been sold—suggests he was more in tune with changes in America than his captious critics. The Beats have given us the most powerful expression in our time of Whitman's candor in the face of a programmed secrecy and control imposed by a governing bureaucratic mentality. As Whitman urged, they have tried to remove the doors, to open the way to a genuine release of feeling.

As a result, they have been credited with the enormous panoply of social change since the end of World War II. Actually, many of the Beats, Kerouac, Burroughs, and Gary Snyder in particular, were often quite detached from painful political immediacies. Writers are observers, rarely activists. As Gary Snyder has maintained, they were interested in moving the world "a millionth of an inch" at a time.

The Beats were part of a generational change that they vigorously proclaimed and to some extent predicted. They have become internationally accepted by readers, particularly young ones. Their legacy has always been spiritual—resistance with the advocacy of art.

Selective Chronology

1914   William Seward Burroughs is born on February 5 in St. Louis, Missouri, second son of Laura Lee, whose family claimed descent from Robert E. Lee, and Mortimer P. Burroughs, whose father had perfected the adding machine.

1915   Herbert Huncke is born on January 9 in Greenfield, Massachusetts. He spent his childhood in Chicago but started leaving home when he was twelve.

1919   Lawrence Ferlinghetti is born on March 24 in Yonkers, New York, the last of five sons of a Portuguese Jewish mother, who was institutionalized when he was an infant, and Charles Ferling, an Italian immigrant auctioneer who died before he was born.

1922   Jean-Louis Lebris de Kerouac is born on March 12 in Lowell, Massachusetts, third child of Gabrielle Ange and Leo Kerouac, French Canadian immigrants to New England.

1926   Neal Cassady is born on February 8 in Salt Lake City to Maude, a lean, angular beauty with seven children from a previous marriage, and Neal Sr., an alcoholic barber who ended up on the Denver bowery.

Allen Ginsberg is born on June 3 in Newark, New Jersey, second son of Naomi, a Russian immigrant, and Louis, a lyric poet and high school English teacher.

1930   Gregory Corso is born on March 26 in New York City to an Italian mother, who abandoned him before he was one, and an Italian father, who abused him until he ran away at the age of thirteen.

Gary Snyder is born on May 8 in San Francisco to Lois Wilkie, descendant of a pioneer family, and Harold Alton Snyder, a marginal farmer.

1936   Burroughs graduates from Harvard.

1940   Kerouac begins playing football at Columbia University.

1943   Ginsberg begins studies at Columbia, has noted critic Lionel Trilling for freshman English, and meets classmate Lucien Carr.

1944   Kerouac meets Ginsberg and Burroughs. Carr murders David Kammarer, who accosted him in Riverside Park. Burroughs and Kerouac collaborate on "And the Hippoes Were Boiled in Their Tanks," an unpublished detective story on the murder.

1945   Burroughs meets Herbert Huncke, who introduces him to morphine and heroin. Ginsberg, suspended from Columbia University, moves to an apartment at 419 West 115th Street near Columbia University with Burroughs, Kerouac, Joan Vollmer Adams, and Edie Parker.

1946   Burroughs is arrested on a drug misdemeanor, receives a suspended sentence. Kerouac, caring for his dying father in Queens, begins *The Town and the City*. Meets Neal Cassady and his sixteen-year-old wife, LuAnne.

1947   Burroughs buys a farm in New Waverly, Texas, and has a son with Joan Vollmer. Kerouac and Ginsberg travel to Denver in pursuit of Neal Cassady. Huncke, Cassady, and Ginsberg visit Burroughs in Texas. Ferlinghetti is enrolled in an M.A. program at Columbia University. Robert Frank comes to America to work for *Harper's Bazaar*.

1948   Kerouac meets John Clellon Holmes, invents term "Beat Generation," begins first version of *On the Road*. Ginsberg experiences Blake vision in East Harlem. Burroughs and Joan Vollmer move to Algiers, outside New Orleans. Kerouac takes his first trip with Cassady.

1949   Ginsberg is admitted to Columbia Psychiatric Institute, where Carl Solomon is his ward mate. Kerouac, Cassady, and LuAnne visit Burroughs in New Orleans. Burroughs is arrested on a drug charge in New Orleans, moves to Mexico City. Ferlinghetti is writing doctoral dissertation on the city in modern poetry at the Sorbonne.

1950   Kerouac's first novel, *The Town and the City,* is published. Snyder lives with Philip Whalen and Lew Welch at Reed College. Released from Columbia Psychiatric, Ginsberg lives with his father in Paterson, New Jersey, and meets William Carlos Williams. Burroughs begins *Junky*, sends manuscript to Ginsberg. Ginsberg meets Corso at the Pony Stable, a Greenwich Village lesbian bar. Ferlinghetti begins attending Kenneth Rexroth's anarchist meetings in San Francisco.

1951   Barney Rosset starts Grove Press. Kerouac writes *On the Road* and begins another version of it with the more experimental *Visions of Cody*. Burroughs shoots Joan Vollmer in Mexico City and works on *Junky*.

1952   Kerouac lives with Carolyn and Neal Cassady in San Francisco, writes "October in the Railroad Earth," and works as a brakeman. Writes *Dr. Sax* in the hall bathroom of Burroughs's apartment in Mexico City. Ginsberg sends William Carlos Williams a group of poems, and gives manuscript of *Junky* to Carl Solomon, who persuades his uncle to publish it. Scribner's publishes John Clellon Holmes's *Go*, and Holmes's article "This Is the Beat Generation" appears in the *New York Times Magazine*.

1953   *Junky* is published pseudonymously as a 35-cent Ace paperback and sells over 100,000 copies in its first year. Burroughs travels in Central and South America and then moves to Tangier. Kerouac writes *Maggie Cassidy* and *The Subterraneans*, and Malcolm Cowley recommends that Viking Press accept *On the Road.*

1954   Kerouac intensively studies Buddhism in New York and California, writes *Some of the Dharma* and *San Francisco Blues.* Michael McClure moves to San Francisco. Burroughs settles in Tangier. Ginsberg travels in Mexico and moves to San Francisco.

1955   Ginsberg meets Peter Orlovsky and writes "Howl for Carl Solomon," which he reads at the Six Gallery along with Gary Snyder, Michael McClure, Philip Whalen, and Philip Lamantia. Kerouac begins *Tristessa* in Mexico City and finishes *Mexico City Blues.* Ferlinghetti starts City Lights Bookstore and Publishers and offers to publish *Howl.*

1956   City Lights publishes *Howl.* Snyder leaves for Japan. Kerouac spends sixty-three days as fire-watcher at Desolation Peak and begins *Desolation Angels* in Mexico City, where he is joined by Ginsberg, Orlovsky, and Corso.

1957   *On the Road* is published. Kerouac, Ginsberg, and Orlovsky travel to Tangier to help Burroughs with *Naked Lunch.* Barney Rosset begins *Evergreen Review. Howl* is seized by U.S. Customs in San Francisco, Ferlinghetti is tried for publishing obscenity, and Judge Clayton Horn rules that *Howl* is not obscene. Robert Frank meets Jack Kerouac in New York and asks him to write an introduction to *The Americans.*

1958   Grove Press publishes *The Subterraneans* and Viking *The Dharma Bums.* New Directions publishes Ferlinghetti's *A Coney Island of the Mind.* City Lights publishes Corso's *Gasoline.* Hettie and LeRoi Jones begin the literary magazine *Yugen.* Burroughs moves to Paris. An excerpt from *Naked Lunch* appears in *Chicago Review,* and is censored. Living Theatre actors renovate a men's department store on Fourteenth Street for a permanent home. Hettie Jones works for *Partisan Review* and tries to introduce writing by the Beats. In the *San Francisco Chronicle,* columnist Herb Caen invents term "beatnik."

1959   The magazine *Big Table* is seized by the U.S. Post Office for publishing a *Naked Lunch* excerpt. Olympia Press in Paris publishes *Naked Lunch.* Gysin and Burroughs begin cut-ups. Ginsberg writes "Kaddish." New Directions releases a selection of Kerouac's *Visions of Cody. Dr. Sax* is published by Grove and *Maggie Cassidy* as an Avon paperback. *Beatitude* magazine is begun in San Francisco. Robert Frank films *Pull My Daisy,* for which Kerouac provides a spontaneous narration.

1960   *Minutes to Go,* cut-ups by Burroughs, Gysin, and Corso, is published.

Grove Press publishes Donald Allen's anthology *The New American Poetry*. Kerouac's *Tristessa* and *Lonesome Traveller* are published. New Directions publishes Corso's *The Happy Birthday of Death* and Ferlinghetti's *Her*. Timothy Leary takes psilocybin mushrooms in Cuernavaca, Mexico, and introduces Ginsberg to them.

1961 City Lights publishes Ginsberg's *Kaddish and other Poems*, and he travels to India with Orlovsky. Kerouac works on *Desolation Angels* in Mexico City and *Big Sur* in Florida. Diane di Prima and LeRoi Jones edit *Floating Bear*. Jones's *Preface to a Twenty Volume Suicide Note* is published. Burroughs's *The Soft Machine* is published by Olympia Press in Paris.

1962 Grove Press publishes *Naked Lunch* and Kerouac's *Big Sur*. New Directions publishes Corso's *Long Live Man*.

1963 *Naked Lunch* obscenity trial takes place in Boston. City Lights publishes Burroughs and Ginsberg's *The Yage Letters*. New Directions publishes Ferlinghetti's *Unfair Arguments with Existence*. Morrow publishes LeRoi Jones's *Blues People*.

1964 Grove publishes Burroughs's *Nova Express*. Morrow publishes Jones's *Dutchman and the Slave*. Kerouac moves to Tampa, Florida, with his mother, sees Cassady for the last time in New York City. Gary Snyder returns from Japan. Internal Revenue Service closes The Living Theatre and its actors flee to Europe.

1965 Michael McClure's *The Beard* is performed by the Actor's Workshop in San Francisco. Ginsberg travels in Cuba, Russia, Poland, and Czechoslovakia, where students crown him "King of May" and he is expelled. Kerouac travels to France and writes *Satori in Paris* in Florida. *Desolation Angels* is published by Coward-McCann. Snyder publishes *Riprap & Cold Mountain Poems* and returns to Japan.

1966 Burroughs settles in London. Kerouac marries Stella Sampas, sister of a childhood friend.

1967 Snyder, Ferlinghetti, McClure, and Ginsberg participate in San Francisco Human Be-In. Kerouac writes *Vanity of Duluoz* in Lowell.

1968 Neal Cassady dies in San Miguel de Allende, Mexico. Burroughs and Ginsberg attend Democratic National Convention in Chicago. The Living Theatre returns for national tour of *Paradise Now*. Kerouac moves to St. Petersburg, Florida.

1969 Kerouac dies on October 21, and is buried in Lowell.

Selected Bibliography

Allen, Donald, ed. *The New American Poetry 1945–1960*. New York: Grove Press, 1960.

———, ed. *The Poetics of the New American Poetry*. New York: Grove Press, 1973.

Amram, David. *Vibrations*. New York: Viking, 1968.

Bartlett, Lee, ed. *The Beats: Essays in Criticism*. Jefferson, N.C.: McFarland, 1981.

Beck, Julian. *The Life of the Theatre*. San Francisco: City Lights Books, 1972.

Bowles, Paul. *Without Stopping: An Autobiography*. New York: Putnam's, 1972.

Burroughs, William S. *Junky: Confessions of an Unredeemed Drug Addict*. New York: Ace Books, 1953.

———. *Naked Lunch*. New York: Grove Press, 1959.

———. *The Job: Interviews with William Burroughs*. Ed. Daniel Odier. New York: Grove Press, 1972.

———. *Cities of the Red Night*. New York: Holt, Rinehart and Winston, 1981.

———. *The Letters of William S. Burroughs, 1945–1959*. Ed. Oliver Harris. New York: Viking, 1993.

Cassady, Carolyn. *Off the Road: My Years with Cassady, Kerouac, and Ginsberg*. New York: Morrow, 1990.

Cassady, Neal. *The First Third*. San Francisco: City Lights Books, 1971.

Charters, Ann, ed. *The Beats: Literary Bohemians in Postwar America*. Ann Arbor: Gale Research, 1983.

———. *Kerouac: A Biography*. San Francisco: Straight Arrow Books, 1973.

———, ed. *The Portable Beat Reader*. New York: Viking, 1992.

Corso, Gregory. *Gasoline*. San Francisco: City Lights Books, 1958.

———. *Elegiac Feelings American*. New York: New Directions, 1970.

Creeley, Robert. *Selected Poems*. New York: Scribner's, 1976.

Davidson, Michael. *The San Francisco Renaissance*. New York: Cambridge University Press, 1989.

Dickstein, Morris. *Gates of Eden*. New York: Basic Books, 1977.

Di Prima, Diane. *Memoirs of a Beatnik*. Paris: Olympia Press, 1969.

Ferlinghetti, Lawrence. *A Coney Island of the Mind*. New York: New Directions, 1958.

————. *These Are My Rivers: New and Selected Poems*. New York: New Directions, 1994.

Frank, Robert. *The Americans*. Introduction by Jack Kerouac. New York: Grove Press, 1959.

Gifford, Barry, and Lawrence Lee. *Jack's Book: An Oral Biography of Jack Kerouac*. New York: St. Martin's Press, 1978.

Ginsberg, Allen. *As Ever: The Collected Correspondence of Allen Ginsberg and Neal Cassady*. Ed. Barry Gifford. Berkeley: Creative Arts, 1977.

————. *Allen Verbatim: Lectures on Poetry, Politics, Consciousness*. Ed. Gordon Ball. New York: McGraw-Hill, 1974.

————. *Collected Poems: 1947–80*. New York: Harper & Row, 1984.

————. *Howl: Original Draft Facsimile Transcript and Variant Versions*. Ed. Barry Miles. New York: Harper & Row, 1986.

————. *Journals Mid-Fifties: 1954–1958*. Ed. Gordon Ball. New York: Harper-Collins, 1995.

Gysin, Brion, with William S. Burroughs. *The Third Mind*. New York: Viking, 1978.

Halper, Jon, ed. *Gary Snyder: Dimensions of a Life*. San Francisco: Sierra Club Books, 1991.

Hamalian, Linda. *A Life of Kenneth Rexroth*. New York: Norton, 1991.

Holmes, John Clellon. *Nothing More to Declare*. New York: Dutton, 1967.

————. *Gone in October: Last Reflections on Jack Kerouac*. Hailey, Idaho: Limberlost Press, 1985.

Huncke, Herbert. *The Herbert Huncke Reader*. Ed. Benjamin Schafer. New York: Morrow, 1997.

Hyde, Lewis, ed. *On the Poetry of Allen Ginsberg*. Ann Arbor: University of Michigan Press, 1984.

Johnson, Joyce. *Minor Characters*. Boston: Houghton Mifflin, 1983.

Jones, Hettie. *How I Became Hettie Jones*. New York: Dutton, 1990.

Jones, LeRoi. *The LeRoi Jones Amiri Baraka Reader*. Ed. William J. Harris. New York: Thunder's Mouth Press, 1995.

Kazin, Alfred, ed. *Writers at Work: The Paris Review Interviews, Third Series*. Conrad Knickerbocker's "Interview with William Burroughs" and Thomas Clark's "Interview with Allen Ginsberg." New York: Viking, 1967.

Kerouac, Jack. *On the Road*. New York: Viking, 1957.

————. *The Subterraneans*. New York: Grove Press, 1958.

————. *Scattered Poems*. San Francisco: City Lights Books, 1971.

————. *Visions of Cody*. New York: McGraw-Hill, 1972.

———. *The Portable Jack Kerouac*. Ed. Ann Charters. New York: Viking, 1995.

———. *Selected Letters: 1940–1956*. Ed. Ann Charters. New York: Viking, 1995.

Kerouac, Jan. *Baby Driver*. New York: St. Martin's Press, 1981.

Kesey, Ken. *The Further Inquiry*. New York: Viking, 1990.

Kinsey, Alfred C. *Sexual Behavior in the Human Male*. Philadelphia: W. B. Saunders, 1948.

Knight, Arthur and Kit. *Kerouac and the Beats*. Foreword by John Tytell and containing his interviews with William S. Burroughs and John Clellon Holmes. New York: Paragon House, 1988.

Knight, Brenda, ed. *The Women of the Beat Generation*. Berkeley: Conari, 1996.

Krim, Seymour. *What's This Cat's Story?* New York: Paragon House, 1991.

Lawlor, William. *The Beat Generation: A Bibliographical Teaching Guide*. Lanham, Md.: Scarecrow Press, 1998.

Leary, Timothy. *Flashbacks: An Autobiography*. Los Angeles: Jeremy Tarcher, 1983.

McClure, Michael. *Scratching the Beat Surface*. San Francisco: North Point Press, 1982.

———. *Selected Poems*. New York: New Directions, 1986.

Mailer, Norman. *The White Negro*. San Francisco: City Lights Books, 1958.

Malina, Judith. *The Diaries of Judith Malina: 1947–1957*. New York: Grove Press, 1984.

Morgan, Ted. *Literary Outlaw: The Life and Times of William S. Burroughs*. New York: Henry Holt, 1988.

Nicosia, Gerald. *Memory Babe: A Critical Biography of Jack Kerouac*. New York: Grove Press, 1983.

Norse, Harold. *Memoirs of a Bastard Angel*. New York: Morrow, 1989.

Orlovsky, Peter. *Clean Asshole Poems & Smiling Vegetable Songs*. San Francisco: City Lights Books, 1978.

Patterson, James. *Grand Expectations*. New York: Oxford University Press, 1996.

Phillips, Lisa. *Beat Culture and the New America 1950–1965*. New York: Whitney Museum of American Art, 1995.

Rivers, Larry, with Arnold Weinstein. *What Did I Do?* New York: HarperCollins, 1992.

Rosset, Barney, ed. *The Evergreen Review Reader, 1957–61*. New York: Grove Press, 1979.

Sanders, Ed. *Investigative Poetry*. San Francisco: City Lights Books, 1976.

Sayre, Nora. *Previous Convictions: A Journal Through the 1950s*. New Brunswick, N.J.: Rutgers University Press, 1995.

Schumacher, Michael. *Dharma Lion: A Biography of Allen Ginsberg*. New York: St. Martin's Press, 1992.

Skerl, Jennie, and Robin Lydenberg, eds. *William S. Burroughs at the Front: Critical Reception, 1959–1989*. Carbondale: Southern Illinois University Press, 1991.

Snyder, Gary. *The Back Country*. New York: New Directions, 1968.

————. *Earth House Hold: Technical Notes & Queries to Fellow Dharma Revolutionaries*. New York: New Directions, 1969.

————. *Mountains and Rivers Without End*. Washington, D.C.: Counterpoint, 1996.

Sobieszek, Robert A. *Ports of Entry: William S. Borroughs and the Arts*. Los Angeles: Los Angeles County Museum of Art, 1996.

Solomon, Carl. *Mishaps, Perhaps*. San Francisco: City Lights Books, 1966.

————. *Emergency Messages: An Autobiographical Miscellany*. Ed. John Tytell. New York: Paragon House, 1989.

Thompson, Hunter S. *The Proud Highway: The Fear and Loathing Letters 1955–1967*. Ed. Douglas Brinkley. New York: Villard, 1997.

Tonkinson, Carol, ed. *Big Sky Mind: Buddhism and the Beat Generation*. New York: Riverhead Books, 1995.

Trungpa, Chogyam. *First Thought Best Thought*. Boston: Shambhala Publications, 1983.

Tytell, John. "On Burroughs's Work: A Conversation with Allen Ginsberg." *Partisan Review* 41, No. 2 (1974).

————. "The Beats Go On." *Vanity Fair*, January 1985.

————. *Naked Angels: The Lives and Literature of the Beat Generation*. New York: McGraw-Hill, 1976. Paperback, New York: Grove Press, 1986.

————. *The Living Theatre: Art, Exile and Outrage*. New York: Grove Press, 1995.

————. "An Interview with William Burroughs." In *The Burroughs Compendium*. Mystic, Conn.: Hozomeen Press, 1998.

Waldman, Anne. *Helping the Dreamer: New and Selected Poems 1966–1988*. Minneapolis: Coffee House Press, 1989.

————. *The Beat Book*. Boston: Shambhala, 1996.

Warren, Holly George. *The Rolling Stone Book of the Beats*. New York: Hyperion, 1999.

Index

Page numbers in *italics* refer to illustrations.

Sanders, Ed, 162, *163,* 212
Scratching the Beat Surface, 48–49, 196p
Smith, Patti, 110, 182, 185, 200, *201,* 210
Snyder, Gary, 22, 48, 60, 62, 74, 90, 113, 180, 189, 196–197, 198, 215
Solomon, Carl, 12, 21, 32, *33,* 40, *41,* 54–55, 84–85, *85,* 176, *177,* 181–182, 186, 198
Some of the Dharma, 64, 142, 154–155, 207
"Song of Myself," 141, 178, 183, 213
Spengler, Oswald, 7, 132, 194
Stein, Gertrude, 30, 76, 124

Subterraneans, The, 84, 119, 129, 134, 138, 196, 213

Thompson, Hunter S., 160, *161,* 208
Thoreau, Henry David, 58, 146, 154
Town and the City, The, 15, 42, 131, 139, 150, 153
Trilling, Diana, 24, 195
Trilling, Lionel, 6, 17–18, 23
Tropic of Cancer, 24, 128, 147, 212
Truman, Harry S., 45–46, 50–51, 53
Tytell, John, 2, *3,* 19–25, 26, *27,* 32, *33,* 40, *41,* 57, 59, 70, 74, *75,* 133, 189–199

Vanity of Dulouz, 20, 150, 152
Visions of Cody, 21, 66, 82, 136–137, 143, 153, 158, 179, 192, 194, 196, 207
Vollmer, Joan, 11–12, 78, 104, 106–107, 119

Waldman, Anne, 72, 88, *89,* 113, 199, 202, *203*
Warhol, Andy, 110, 111, 171
Whitman, Walt, 8, 9, 61–62, 132, 140–142, 178, 182, 183, 197–198, 206, 213, 215
Williams, William Carlos, 6, 26, 74, 197

Young, Lester, 8, 135, 184, 211